Trojan Horse

Trojan Horse

Natural Rights and America's Founding

Ruben Alvarado

WordBridge
PUBLISHING
εν αρχη ην ο λογος
AALTEN, THE NETHERLANDS

WORDBRIDGE PUBLISHING
Aalten, the Netherlands
www.wordbridge.net
info@wordbridge.net

Copyright © 2022 Ruben Alvarado

ISBN 978–90–76660–69–1

COVER ILLUSTRATION: "Declaration of Independence" by John Trumbull (1819), depicting the five-man drafting committee of the Declaration of Independence presenting their work to the Congress. The original hangs in the US Capitol rotunda. This representation is in the public domain. The clipart rendition of the Trojan Horse is likewise in the public domain.

TABLE OF CONTENTS

INTRODUCTION

As we approach the 250th anniversary of the signing of the Declaration of Independence, we are once again confronted with the conundrum the Declaration poses. It states as self-evident truths that "all men are created equal," that they are "endowed by their Creator with certain inalienable rights," that "among these are Life, Liberty and the pursuit of Happiness"; that civil government is instituted "to secure these rights," and that governments derive "their just powers from the consent of the governed."

If we are to believe that these portentious phrases apply to all human beings equally, then we indeed have a conundrum on our hands. Take, for example, restrictions on immigration. These restrictions revolve around the concept that foreign citizens do not have the rights US citizens have; in particular, they do not have the right to enter and reside in the US. The champions of open immigration make just that point, their position being that such restrictions imply that all men are *not* created equal, that they do *not* equally enjoy certain inalienable rights, among which the pursuit of happiness, which is what immigrants to the US seek above all things.

So if we were to take the Declaration seriously, we would open our borders wide. Just as in 1776 – if those phrases had really been believed and taken literally, the slaves would have to have been freed immediately. But they weren't.

The same thing is true regarding the restrictions on sexuality in favor of traditional marriage and the family. Say what you will about Supreme Court Justice Anthony Kennedy, in his jurisprudence regarding homosexuality and marriage as expressed in the majority opinion re Obergefell v. Hodges, he was simply being faithful to these same portentious phrases.

The recent decision in the case of Dobbs v. Jackson, in which the Supreme Court overturned Roe v. Wade and ruled that the Court does not have jurisdiction over abortion, would seem to reverse that. It appears that not all justices follow this reasoning. They stick to the explicit text of the Constitution only, rather than resort to the logic implicit in the Declaration. But the minority opinion as expressed by Justices Breyer, Kagan, and Sotomayor minces no words in condemning that approach. The jurisprudence as expressed in Roe v. Wade is simply the reflection of changed cultural and societal conditions. Of course there is no express provision of a right to abortion in the Constitution. After all, women were considered second-class citizens without freedom of choice regarding their bodies and health decisions.

The progressives are only having the jurisprudence of the Constitution catch up with the text of the Declaration. This is why such issues are cast as inevitable. To be in favor of same-sex marriage, then, is to be "on the right side of history."[1] To be opposed is to be as retrograde as it is to be opposed to human rights generally. It is no good to refer to millennia of contradictory human history, to self-evident laws of nature, to the teaching of all religions everywhere, to the teaching of the Christian church, to which the majority of persons in the United States still professes to adhere, to the teaching of Scripture. None of that matters, because "history" is on the side of "gay" marriage.

What explains this inevitability? Quite simply, the natural

---

[1] It is quite odd on the one hand to see this line of reasoning pushed so vociferously, and yet, on the other, to see precedent (stare decisis!) equally vociferously maintained once a desired position is attained – even though that position be utterly novel, overthrowing, as in the case of same-sex marriage, thousands of years of precedent.

rights paradigm that is enshrined in the Declaration. As we shall see, this paradigm was placed at the heart of Western legal and political institutions back in the 17th century. That's right: the document signed nearly 250 years ago ratified the state of affairs that would eventually produce things like same-sex marriage.

Of course, we may presume that the Founders would be rolling in their graves if they had known that this would be the end-result of their work. Which would seem to be *prima facie* evidence against this thesis. But a short explanation of the mechanics will elucidate our meaning and confirm it.

Time and again, the justification for all of these jurisprudential "advances" is found in the 14th Amendment to the US Constitution. On the face of it, it seems odd that the rights-ore that the Court has mined from the Constitution, it has mined from this text. The language is standard Lockean phraseology: rights to life, liberty, and property, along with a right to due process of law in adjudicating those rights; and that these rights accrue to every American citizen, either naturalized or born on US soil. How is it that rights of such divergent import (e.g., privacy justifying a right to abortion, same-sex marriage, non-citizen welfare benefits), having nothing to do with the ones here enumerated, nevertheless have been teased out of this?

It is because an enumeration of rights presupposes a mechanism of rights from which the enumerated rights have been derived; it is the mechanism which matters, standing as it does, over and above any listed enumeration and any law which might presume to contradict it. And this is what generation after generation of Supreme Court justices has divined.

What is this mechanism? The mechanism of natural rights, precisely the intellectual leaven taken up in the Declaration, which has served to leaven the whole lump of national dough.

The dissenters to Dobbs v. Jackson argue precisely this. The notion that changing conditions necessitate changed laws and a changing understanding of the Constitution was understood, they argue, by both its framers and the framers of the 14th Amendment – for which reason they resorted to a rights mechanism (now known as "substantive due process") above and beyond enumerated specifics. "The Framers (both in 1788 and 1868) understood that the world changes. So they did not define rights by reference to the specific practices existing at the time. Instead, the Framers defined rights in general terms, to permit future evolution in their scope and meaning. And over the course of our history, this Court has taken up the Framers' invitation. It has kept true to the Framers' principles by applying them in new ways, responsive to new societal understandings and conditions."[2] The natural-rights paradigm as expressed in the Declaration and which gained entry to the Constitution via the 14th Amendment is the *fons et origo* of the judicial activism which has rendered the Constitution a wax nose.

That is what we will explore in this book. And we will explore its application in the three areas that serve as pillars of the social order: economics, politics (broadly speaking, thus matters concerning "the polity"), and religion.

We will also explore the alternative, which we characterize as the common-law order. Such an order is based on the notion that liberty is not a pre-existing condition, something which just happens to be there, and which is simply to be preserved intact by civil government – something to which all are entitled by virtue of their bare existence – but rather a birthright, an inheritance, an heirloom. It is the product of centuries of labor within the context of specifically Western Christian civilization. Nor was its development any sort of blind process; it was the fruit of the deliberate emphasis on establishing a civilization upon fundamental principles both theological

---

[2] *Dobbs v. Jackson,* 597 U. S. (2022), dissent, p. 16.

and judicial. Western civilization, then, is Christian civilization, but more specifically it is Roman-Christian civilization, which explains why "law" could be one of the deciding criteria in its definition. The Western emphasis on law, and specifically on the notion of a "common" law, underlies the development of its unique heritage of liberty. And in the inexorable course of history, this common-law tradition now maintains a precarious existence indeed.

Let us turn to examine this in more detail.

POLITICS

Contemporary American politics, especially conservative politics, is ruled by the idea of natural rights as incorporated in the Declaration of Independence.[3] In contemporary debate, reference is made to the natural right of life, the natural right of liberty, the natural right to pursue happiness, which, as the Declaration of Independence states, is the reason for which governments were instituted, and the reason why government should not make any laws infringing such rights.

I will characterize this as "State of Nature Politics." For its roots lie in the concept of an original "state of nature," whereby civil government is seen to have originated in a so-called social contract. This approach was pioneered in the 17th century by the Dutch jurist Hugo Grotius and, with some modifications, was furthered by John Locke.

Escape from Christian Confession

Why was this newfangled doctrine adopted? In what consisted its attraction? For Grotius, it came as an answer to the wars of religion – the 80 Years' War between Spain and the Netherlands and, at the tail end thereof, the 30 Years' War in Germany. As he wrote in 1625, "Throughout the Christian world I observed a lack of restraint in relation to war, such as even barbarous races should be ashamed of; I observed that men rush to arms for slight causes, or no cause at all, and that when arms have once been taken up there is no longer any respect for law, divine or human; it is as if, in accordance with a general decree, frenzy had openly been let loose for the

---

[3] See my *Common Law & Natural Rights* for further details on this point.

committing of all crimes."[4] To bring about this restraint, Grotius was concerned to discover the basis for the authority of civil government – in other words, sovereignty – apart from divine right. The wars of religion, he was convinced, had made this basis untenable, for divine right required acknowledgment of a particular religion, and thus precluded adherents of various faiths from living together in peace.

Grotius felt he had discovered a more secure basis on the purely human plane of contract. Law, he stated, was the expression of strict justice, and thus the stuff of contract and property. And for him, contract was even prior to property, for property itself, the division of the goods of the earth, was the result of human agreement. And governments were formed in like manner, by a primordial agreement through which sovereignty was formed by the delegation and in fact alienation of the sword-power which each individual has from nature.

John Locke adapted Grotius' basic approach but changed it in significant ways. Firstly, he made property to be dependent not upon a hypothetical agreement but simply upon a natural right derived from each individual's own labor. That which an individual appropriated or created by his own labor was by the law of nature his own (see page 32 below). Thus, property cannot be undone by agreement. Furthermore, governments were formed by the delegation of the power of the sword, but this delegation did not entail alienation. Every man retained the right of resistance, the right to bear arms, and in fact the government's power of the sword is simply a delegation of this primordial right.[5]

---

[4] *De Jure Belli ac Pacis Libri Tres* [On the Law of War and Peace], Prolegomena 28, p. 20.

[5] The trajectory of this system from Grotius to Locke is described in my

This line of reasoning would seem to provide the citizen with a solid rationale for insisting on limited government and on the necessity for government to consult with its citizens and ensure that the laws it passes and enforces correspond with the will of the citizenry. Furthermore, that these laws serve to protect these basic natural rights which in fact, at least in the Lockean approach as continued by the Declaration of Independence, stand even beyond the reach of the will of the people, are inalienable and sacrosanct, by virtue of being established by God, whose will is prior to the will of any man, individual or collective.

There is a fly in the ointment, however, at least for those who do not believe in human autonomy but in the primacy of God's will and law not only for one's private affairs but also for human life in society. And it is this: the philosophy of natural rights makes human nature into the source of law, with God only coming into the picture as the instiller of such "natural law" in human nature.[6]

The key at this point becomes interpretation. What comprises the range of obligations the government is charged to uphold? The doctrine opens a Pandora's box of conflicting opinion and chaos precisely where settled legal foundations are required. If natural rights are the source of law, then laws ultimately will be subjected to the philosophical opinions of the judge. It is precisely at this point that F. J. Stahl directed his major criticism of this school of thought. "The application of natural law in the courtroom is ... impermissible legally, is contrary to justice. Every man has the right not to be

---

Calvin and the Whigs, while a detailed exploration of Grotius' system is found in my *The Debate that Changed the West.*

[6] "§ 11: The natural law is not dependent on God for its content, nor for its existence, but only for its implantation in us. It would exist even if God did not exist." Grotius, *De Jure Belli ac Pacis,* in *The Debate that Changed the West,* p. 200.

subjected to any other norm than those which are established as the objective order of the common life, which are sanctioned by the ruling authorities, as the norms of positive law."[7] In other words, everyone has the right to know the law beforehand. But natural rights doctrine gives the judge a blank check, allowing him to strike down any law he believes contradicts natural rights. "The rule of natural law is therefore in truth only the establishment of the arbitrariness of every opinion regarding the common public order, it is the establishment of the war of all against all."[8]

The attempt to integrate the concept of human nature into the philosophy of law is praiseworthy, but it must be done properly. The history of the development of the philosophy of natural rights demonstrates this. Jurists and theologians realized the importance of anthropology to legal philosophy, and developed the concept of *subjective right*, or law in the subjective sense, which pins down the place of the *legal subject,* i.e., personality, in the formation of law. Stahl summarizes:

> Accordingly, law in the subjective sense is the *ethical power* which a man has over against others in the sphere allotted to him by the legal order, by virtue of that order. Its essence is not merely the negative of allowance or the intransitive of freedom, but the positive and transitive of ethical power against others.
>
> Law in the subjective sense, e.g., the right of men due him in all his life positions, constructs, in that it is his own power inhering in him, a true center about which the entire external world (things, actions of others, etc.) is related as controlled object, and in accordance with which the content of legal norms is often determined. It is therefore a *secondary principle of the legal order* alongside the

---

[7] Stahl, *Principles of Law,* p. 37.

[8] Stahl, *Principles of Law,* p. 38.

primary and absolute principle: the *purpose* (τέλος) of *life relations.* As secondary principle, however, it is always based upon this latter. Its own content and range is originally and essentially derived from, and the coherence of all the rights of all men lies in, this objective higher principle.[9]

There is therefore a law-conditioning principle inherent in human nature, rooted in man's creation in the image of God, stemming from his capacity to reason and choose, his capacity for ethical activity. It calls for a sphere of activity to be established on his behalf within the legal order and protected by that legal order. The specific content of that sphere is more closely determined by the legal order in accordance with the institutions of law (marriage, family, property, etc.).

Hence, a "sphere of influence" is called for regarding each individual human being. This is what is put forward in the doctrine of subjective right; but the specific content of that sphere is the province of positive law, to be determined in terms of the various factors of the human condition.

The Genesis of Rights[10]

Now then, the Christian confesses a peculiar understanding of the human condition, one which is anthropological although cosmological as well: the human condition as fallen, corrupted, sinful. This factor is of decisive importance to the development of a legal order.

Roman jurists, following in the footsteps of Stoic philosophers, had postulated an original "golden age" in which all men were equal,

---

[9] Stahl, *Principles of Law,* pp. 99–101.

[10] The following discussion can be supplemented with the chapters "Origins" and "Establishment" in my *Calvin and the Whigs.*

all men were free, in which there was no war, no subjection, and no private property, no *meum et tuum*, "mine and thine." This was the age of the natural law. But then, they said, there came the age of the *jus gentium* ("law of nations"), which brought all of these things into being.

This is how Justinian's *Institutes* (Book I, Title II, §. 2) states the matter:

> The Law of Nations... is common to the entire human race, for all nations have established for themselves certain regulations exacted by custom and human necessity. For wars have arisen, and captivity and slavery, which are contrary to natural law, have followed as a result, as, according to natural law, all men were originally born free; and from this law [i.e., the law of nations] nearly all contracts, such as purchase, sale, hire, partnership, deposit, loan, and innumerable others have been derived.

The Romans therefore understood that a break had occurred at some point in primordial history, a break in which an age of innocence was followed by the age of division, subjection, property, slavery – the various institutions of civilization as then understood. And it would seem from the above quotation that they attributed that break precisely to these institutions, anticipating Rousseau's argument (see p. 55 below).

The Christians knew better. The corruption in the world was cause by man's fall into sin, by his disobedience to God. The consequences were clear, at least to the Roman Christian par excellence, Augustine, and Western theology in his train. The fall into sin was what had given rise to the subjection of man to man, both as punishment for sin and as a restraint on sin's effects. As a result, the prior concept was not liberty, but authority, the recognition and the proper exercise thereof.[11]

The result was what we now know as medieval society. Medieval man knew little of abstract liberty, but he was well acquainted with liberties, entailing the gradual, and graduated, release from the baseline condition of subjection, expressed in the typical hierarchical order progressing from serf to king.

In this new order of the ages (wonder of wonders!) slavery had no place.

> The right of the fully free was, in the middle ages, at bottom essentially the same as the right of the partly free, whereas in antiquity freeman and slave stood in sharpest contrast to each other, the one a person, the other a thing. In the middle ages both were persons, and the rights of both had a similar legal structure. Each possessed a concrete bundle of rights, with corresponding duties. Differences were largely quantitative. The unfree lived under the most widely varying laws, but even the lowest had some rights and were not at their lord's arbitrary disposal. Though bound to the soil, the villein had a claim to his land and could not be separated from it; frequently he had the right only to be judged by his fellow-villeins; and he could only be called upon to do a fixed amount of labour in the fields. Similarly, those who were unfree but not bound to the soil were only liable for limited dues in money and labour. It is characteristic of medieval freedom that it is frequently mentioned in relation to men who were in law either unfree or only partly free; it is common to find the rights of *ministeriales*, *censuales*, or *cerocensuales* described as *libertates*.[12]

The conversion on Christmas Day 496 A.D. of Clovis and the Franks to Roman Christianity ushered in the new order of the ages:

---

[11] See *Calvin and the Whigs,* pp. 10ff.

[12] Tellenbach, *Church, State, and Christian Society,* p. 19.

baptized Trinitarian Western Europe. (Prior to Clovis' fateful decision, unitarian Arianism was a strong alternative.) Baptism received its outworking in the establishment of such a covenantal framework of social bonds regulating liberty and subjection. Within this new framework, there was no rigid distinction between bond and free: all were in bondage to sin, but all were also freed by salvation in Christ; and social bonds reflected the resultant degrees of freedom. There was no longer slave or free, but only a sliding scale of relative freedom and relative bondage. The various forms of feudal bond fleshed out this understanding. Only in this manner could man's basic corruption and sinfulness be kept in check, allowing the development of subjective right, the ever-expanding "sphere of influence" which each individual possesses as a potentiality to be actualized.

The actualization of this potentiality into the concrete shape of legal personality, legal capacity, citizenship, was enabled by sovereignty. Kingship, in which sovereignty found expression, is what allowed feudal society to move forward into a proper property-based, common-law social order. This is obvious in a country like England, where the king's authority for the most part was above dispute, and where his writ ran right across the isle. Matters were different in the Holy Roman Empire, where the emperor was relatively powerless to impose his writ at all. But this confirms rather than obviates the thesis proposed here. With the expansion of associationalism in Italy and the other regions of the Empire, the towns, the centers of that associationalism, found their legitimization in the emperor; and it was his approval, his grant recognizing rights, immunities, privileges, and charters, which created the public-legal framework of authority which could support a complexifying, differentiating social order.

Roman law facilitated this transformation. It filled in the gaps inevitably left where a property-based society with its emphasis on individualism emerges in the midst of a feudal society with its collectivism. Essentially, the collectives were shrinking while the individualities were multiplying, resulting in new forms of association to accommodate the otherwise free-floating individuals. The manor was being transformed from a system of servility to one of freehold, or at least copyhold, tenure, its monolithic introversion being broken up and replaced through openness to an integrating, interdependency-shaping world. Roman law helped shape the institutions of private law regarding external relations between these associations; indigenous law maintained and developed the shape of the internal relations of the associations (see also p. 60 below).

The manor, then, was the physical location in which these bonds were associated, and initially it was the economic hub of the social order. Lord and vassal established rulership over the manor, with the vassal's rule contingent on the lord's grant. The vassal enjoyed its economic provision, which he received in exchange for military services to the lord. The rule of thumb was that a manor should support the fitting out of a knight and his accompanying warhorses and entourage.[13]

The personnel of the manor were likewise engaged in terms of a feudal bond, this time between lord and serf. Even the lowest man on the feudal totem pole enjoyed some level of freedom, and over time this freedom expanded, through a process of give-and-take which was largely determined by economics.

---

[13] "Germans until this century called it a *Rittergut,* a knight's estate, endowed with legal status and economic and political privileges, and containing at least fifty peasant families or some two hundred people to produce the food needed to support the fighting machine: the knight, his squire, his three horses, and his twelve to fifteen grooms." Peter Drucker, *Post-Capitalist Society* (New York: HarperBusiness, 1993), p. 23.

The transformation of the manor heralded the return of economic growth during the medieval renaissance of the 12th century onward. Part of the reason that there had even been Dark Ages was the collapse of the Roman economy in the West, with an accompanying dearth of silver, the fuel of the pre-modern economy. In the 12th century, silver production and thus monetary circulation took flight, precipitating a boom which would last a couple of centuries, and which would likewise fuel the constitutional developments of the age.[14]

And so the manor went from relatively self-sufficient autarchy to the center of the production of an agricultural surplus. This in turn supplied the material basis for the rise of towns and cities.

These economic changes produced changes in status, engendering freedom. The commutation of physical services to money services transformed the lord/serf relationship. The surplus population moved into the towns and cities, where individuals gained the status of citizen. "Stadluft macht frei" (city air makes free) became the order of the day.

Henry Sumner Maine famously described this transformation as the shift from status to contract. By this he meant the shift from varying statuses embodying levels of freedom and privilege, to a single common status, that of citizen, with the center of gravity in human relations shifting toward contractual relations between citizens.

John Rogers Commons spoke of the passage from subjection to liberty as a shift from unreleasable to releasable debts. An unreleasable debt is one that cannot be repaid, and so results in the permanent subjection of the debtor to the creditor: this is the situation of the slave or the serf. A releasable debt, on the other hand, can be

---

[14] For more on the monetary aspect, see my *Follow the Money*, ch. 6, "Reorientation."

repaid by fulfilling the terms of the contract: therefore, the debtor does not fall into the status of permanent subjection, but retains equal status with the creditor.

So then, in the age of subjection, contract (=covenant) determines status; in the age of liberty, status, which is fixed for all (=the citizen), determines contract.

These are the theoretical underpinnings of the genealogy of liberty. The praxis was hashed out in an ever-increasing number of proclamations, charters of rights and liberties, and simple prescription, arduously attained over the centuries by subjects from masters, vassals from lords, estates from monarchs, asymptotically approaching the limit of the status/contract curve. Books such as Perry's *Sources of Our Liberties* chronicle the advance of chartered liberty through the centuries within the Anglo-American sphere, culminating in the US Constitution and Bill of Rights. The result was the Western legal order.

This legal order, developing through the interplay of courts, sovereigns, and jurists with their burgeoning commentaries, formed a unique interplay of unity in diversity. A *Ius Commune* [common law] was fashioned out of the various materials of the Western legal tradition, dominated by the *utriumque ius*, the one-and-the-other – Roman and canon – law, the degree obtained by law students upon culmination of their studies, alongside indigenous customary law, feudal law, manorial law, municipal law, territorial law, admiralty law, and the Law Merchant.[15]

The common law has been greatly misunderstood. Its role has been seen chiefly as a subsidiary form of positive law, and therefore

---

[15] Berman, *Law and Revolution,* provides a helpful overview of these various forms of law, although it falls short in describing the common law. That shortcoming is made up for in Bellomo, *The Common Legal Past of Europe, 1000–1800*.

its importance has been de-emphasized, in tandem with the tendency to de-emphasize the importance of the Holy Roman Empire simply because the lack of direct political power on the part of the Emperor, along with the obvious datum that most of the countries in Europe were independent. But this is to misconstrue its role. It was never to provide a direct, positive legal order, but rather an atmosphere, a way of thinking, a form of general equity to be used to assist in the formation of positive law.[16]

This common law entered the life of the nations comprising Western civilization, pressing forward to inspire positive legal orders incorporating the universal integrating principles of law, an order wherein private law strings the beads of an expanding associationalism, allowing for the growth of diversified, pluralistic society of communities, of unity in diversity.

The twin poles of this growth were custom and prescription. Custom refers to law; prescription, to rights. The objective order of law developed primarily through custom, thus spontaneously via recognition by the courts; the subjective order of rights developed through the mechanism of prescription, liberties accruing through the passage of time, passed on from generation to generation, in similar fashion to property itself, for having once been attained, such liberties could not be removed again without cause, even if the original "title deed" were no longer available – for the significance of prescription is that it provides security of property in the absence of title, as a result of continuous possession.

As such, this body of rights and liberties developed historically,

---

[16] A point Bellomo makes in *The Common Legal Past of Europe*. See also F. C. Savigny, *System of the Modern Roman Law,* vol. I, §§. 1 and 2. (An updated, corrected version is available at http://84.80.12.175/commonlaw-review/juridical/savigny-on-principles-of-law.)

and came to be viewed as an inheritance. This can be seen clearly in England, in particular in the 17th century struggles between constitutionalism and absolutism. Christopher Brooke, a leading member of the House of Commons in the early 17th century, put it this way: "We hold our privileges by prescription and prescription is inheritance."[17]

William Penn (1644–1718) placed great stock in this ancient constitution. The rights of Englishmen were a great good: "Above all Kingdoms under Heaven, it is *England's* Felicity to have her Constitution so impartially Just and Free, as there cannot well be any Thing more remote from Arbitrariness, and Zealous of preserving the Laws, by which it's Rights are maintained."[18] Basic to this constitution are fundamental laws, of which the first part is the general principles of the common law of nations,[19] the second the rights of Englishmen:

> But those Rights and Priviledges, which I call *English,* and which are the proper *Birth-Right* of *Englishmen,* and may be reduced to these Three.
>
> I. An Ownership, and Undisturbed Possession: That what they have, is Rightly theirs, and no Body's else.

---

[17] Corinne C. Weston, "England: Ancient Constitution and Common Law," in *The Cambridge History of Political Thought: 1450–1700,* p. 377.

[18] "England's Present Interest Considered," in *The Political Writings of William Penn,* p. 26.

[19] "the Corner-Stones of Humane Structure, the Basis of Reasonable Societies, without which all would run into Heaps and Confusion; to wit, Honestè [*sic*] vivere, Alterum non laedere, jus suum cuique tribuere, that is, To live honestly, not to hurt another, and to give every one their Right, (Excellent Principles, and common to all Nations)." "England's Present Interest Considered," in *The Political Writings of William Penn,* p. 26.

II. A Voting of every Law that is made, whereby that Owner-ship or Propriety may be maintained.

III. An Influence upon, and a Real Share in that Judicatory Power that must apply every such Law, which is the Ancient Necessary and Laudable Use of Juries: If not found among the Britains, to be sure Practised by the Saxons, and continued through the Normans to this very Day.

That these have been the Ancient and Undoubted Rights of Englishmen, as Three great Roots, under whose Spacious Branches the English People have been wont to shelter themselves against the Storms of Arbitrary Government, I shall endeavour to prove.[20]

English rights and liberties were precisely those which established the citizen in his liberty and property, which enabled him to function within the common-law social order. The constitution, the public-legal order, existed to maintain and support this private-legal order.

From Historical to Natural Rights

This ancient constitution was brought over by the Englishmen who founded the New World colonies of Virginia, Massachusetts Bay, and those which followed. Americans were Englishmen, endowed with the rights thereto accruing, and the English common law was the law of the land on both sides of the Atlantic. Such an understanding was reflected in the first of the American revolutionary documents, the *Resolutions of the Stamp Act Congress* of 1765, which declared "That his majesty's subjects in these colonies, owe the same allegiance to the crown of Great Britain, that is owing from his subjects born within the realm, and all due subordination to that

---

[20] "England's Present Interest Considered," in *The Political Writings of William Penn,* pp. 26–27.

august body, the parliament of Great Britain," and, concurrently, "That his majesty's liege subjects in these colonies are entitled to all the inherent rights and privileges of his natural born subjects within the kingdom of Great Britain."

Yet from this point the emphasis shifted drastically. A shift came about beginning in 1774, a shift away from chartered liberties – liberty as inheritance, within the Augustinian framework – and toward the law of nature and inalienable natural rights – liberty as man's natural condition, as if no fall had ever occurred (may we call this Pelagian? If not, why not?).

What happened in 1774? John Adams drily sums it up. During the first Continental Congress, sitting on the committee to draw up a statement of liberties, he reports: "Whether we should recur to the law of nature, as well as to the British constitution, and our American charters and grants. Mr. Galloway and Mr. Duane were for excluding the law of nature. I was very strenuous for retaining and insisting on it, as a resource to which we might be driven by Parliament much sooner than we were aware" (*The Works of John Adams*, vol. 2, p. 374).

But in that case, Mr. Adams, it is no longer a question of inheritance, of laborious acquisition, against the Augustinian backdrop of original subjection, the product of amelioration in terms of a progress in virtue. No, it is now a question of natural rights (which, as Stahl documented,[21] is the modern version of natural law), and wherever they do not obtain, an injustice has been done. And what they even *are* is the open-ended $64 question, the driving force of modern politics.

The Declaration of Independence states of the King of England that "the actions of that monarch were declared to be in violation of the inalienable rights of man; they had as their object the

---

[21] in *The Rise and Fall of Natural Law*.

establishment of an absolute tyranny over the states." As such, "No mention was made... of the rights of Englishmen."[22] By now the leaven of natural rights permeated the American colonies, just as it permeated all of Western civilization. Historical rights had given way to natural rights. On the continent, legal philosophy was being conducted entirely in this key.

England, too, had undergone that influence, but its common law had not been subjected to the codification efforts the legal systems of the continent had been. The inherent conflict between historic and natural rights doctrines was slumbering beneath the surface. It took the outbreak of the French Revolution and Edmund Burke's celebrated response (published as *Reflections on the Revolution in France*) to burst the bubble of harmony. From this point on, the conflict between historic and natural rights was out in the open for all to see.

Burke's critique was scathing. "In the famous law of the 3rd of Charles I, called the *Petition of Right*, the parliament says to the king, 'Your subjects have *inherited* this freedom,' claiming their franchises not on abstract principles 'as the rights of men,' but as the rights of Englishmen, and as a patrimony derived from their forefathers" (p. 37). *Rights are inherited, not natural.* "You will observe that from Magna Charta to the Declaration of Right it has been the uniform policy of our constitution to claim and assert our liberties as an *entailed inheritance* derived to us from our forefathers, and to be transmitted to our posterity – as an estate specially belonging to the people of this kingdom, without any reference whatever to any other more general or prior right" (p. 38).

But the new breed of statesmen has lost touch with this inheritance and has nothing but contempt for a prescriptive constitution.

---

[22] Perry, *Sources of Our Liberties,* p. 318.

It is no wonder, therefore, that with these ideas of everything in their constitution and government at home, either in church or state, as illegitimate and usurped, or at best as a vain mockery, they look abroad with an eager and passionate enthusiasm. Whilst they are possessed by these notions, it is vain to talk to them of the practice of their ancestors, the fundamental laws of their country, the fixed form of a constitution whose merits are confirmed by the solid test of long experience and an increasing public strength and national prosperity. They despise experience as the wisdom of unlettered men; and as for the rest, they have wrought underground a mine that will blow up, at one grand explosion, all examples of antiquity, all precedents, charters, and acts of parliament. They have "the rights of men." Against these there can be no prescription, against these no agreement is binding; these admit no temperament and no compromise; anything withheld from their full demand is so much of fraud and injustice. Against these their rights of men let no government look for security in the length of its continuance, or in the justice and lenity of its administration. The objections of these speculatists, if its forms do not quadrate with their theories, are as valid against such an old and beneficent government as against the most violent tyranny or the greenest usurpation. They are always at issue with governments, not on a question of abuse, but a question of competency and a question of title (p. 68).

"By having a right to everything they want everything" (p. 70). Indeed, we have here the entitlement mentality in the bud. Such is the fruit of the natural rights doctrine. But what we need to realize is this:

> Government is a contrivance of human wisdom to provide for human wants. Men have a right that these wants should be provided for by this wisdom. Among these wants is to be reckoned the want,

out of civil society, of a sufficient restraint upon their passions. Society requires not only that the passions of individuals should be
subjected, but that even in the mass and body, as well as in the individuals, the inclinations of men should frequently be thwarted,
their will controlled, and their passions brought into subjection.
This can only be done *by a power out of themselves*, and not, in the
exercise of its function, subject to that will and to those passions
which it is its office to bridle and subdue (pp. 70–71).

The Augustinian bedrock, so antithetical to the entitlement
mentality, is clear. Burke would have nothing of "the pretended
rights of these theorists," which "are all extremes," which "in proportion as they are metaphysically true, they are morally and politically
false" (p. 73).

A Tale of Two Revolutions

Burke's strictures were directed against the revolutionaries in
France. In America, by contrast, the revolutionaries were not interested in overthrowing the received order; they were interested, rather, in maintaining their received institutions, customs, and laws in
the face of an overweening British monarchy and parliament. But
as we have seen, they provided a new basis for these institutions: the
natural-rights theory originating in Grotius. "Many of the Revolutionary patriots believed with Thomas Dickinson that liberties do
not result from charters; charters rather are in the nature of decla-
rations of pre-existing rights."[23] Yet, although both the American
and the French Revolution partook of the elixir of inalienable natural rights, the underlying constitutions which they established
turned out to be of a fundamentally different sort. Post-revolution-
ary France put paid to its feudal past; America, on the other hand,

---

[23] Haines, *The Revival of Natural Law Concepts*, ch. II, sec. 2.

carried out "a conservative counter-revolution."[24]

Nevertheless, in terms *not* of speculative philosophy but of fact and history, America's (and the West's) true "Declaration of Independence" was nothing other than the outworking of the Gospel as it was carried to our forefathers by the monks and priests of the Roman church during that most eventful, yet misunderstood, period of our history, the Dark Ages. The purveyors of natural liberty conveniently jettisoned that history. They slandered it as the age of "Barbarism and Religion," and, purloined inheritance in hand, went their merry way "proclaiming liberty throughout all the land."

Of course, the champion of natural rights will object that this framework of rights as inheritance makes liberty the creature of government, that the rights and liberties enjoyed by the citizens are the gifts of the sovereign and can therefore be revoked at will by the sovereign. Now it is not to be denied that this common-law system emphasizes the role of positive law and civil institutions as the pillars of liberty, rather than allotting that role to supposed pre-existing rights. But the corollary to this system of positive law and rights is not an absolute law-creating sovereignty. Instead, the corollary to this form of civil liberty is *limited* sovereignty, a sovereignty which discovers the law rather than creates it. This does not mean that such sovereignty also discovers pre-existing rights. Rights are the creatures of law, and not the other way around. What the common-law system does is call the civil magistrate to recognize the legitimate *grounds* for positive civil and political rights, as put forward in the doctrine of subjective right. The specific *content* of those rights, the actual concrete shape subjective right takes in a specific legal context, cannot be determined beforehand but must be delineated in an ongoing process against the background of *both* the goal of

---

[24] Rushdoony, *This Independent Republic,* p. 21. The chapter entitled "Feudalism and Federalism" is enlightening in this regard.

liberty *and* the baseline of sin and its corollary, subjection, hence authority. Rights must be derived within the context of existing positive law, behind which lies the law of God, epitomized in the Decalogue.

It is this process which is the true origin of Western liberty and constitutionalism. The fact is beyond dispute. As we have seen, chartered or prescriptive rights and liberties granted or recognized by the sovereign expanded first in the shape of feudal bonds (vassalage, grounding manorial bonds), later cities and towns, guilds, universities, and in fact all manner of legal persons, individual and corporate alike. Adherence to charters was guaranteed with every new accession to the throne, in the form of the coronation oath.[25] Conflicts between crown and subject with regard to chartered liberties were part and parcel of this process. Out of this grew those liberties.

The natural-rights doctrine was developed and applied after the fact to these institutions of liberty, which were produced without it and which had no need of it. There is no pre-existing liberty on the basis of which a sovereign is then established, so as to guarantee it. Sovereignty is the climate within which liberty can grow; outside of that sphere, there is no liberty, there is anarchy, wherein might makes right.

To summarize: *The American Revolution and its ideological progeny forced a common-law regime onto the Procrustean bed of the natural-rights doctrine.* That inherently unstable juxtaposition has led to a conflictedness, a double-mindedness which does not afflict the heirs of the French Revolution, who see their way clearly: government is the solution to all problems. *Their* solution leads to the overthrow of historic institutions and the impoverishment of law through the establishment of Jacobin institutions, unaccountable

---

[25] See Johannes Althusius, *Politica Methodice Digesta,* ch. XIX (reproduced in *The Debate that Changed the West,* pp. 145–148).

"representation" and bureaucracy, and incessant codification. It has led to the situation today in which these two traditions stand opposed to each other, each claiming to represent Western civilization, indeed world order: the common-law tradition, headed by the United States, and the civil-law tradition, headed by the European Union; indeed, the latter is the ideology of the entire globalist hegemon.[26]

The conflict between these two traditions has taken place mainly at the level of economics, which conveniently is the topic of the next chapter.

---

[26] This is the theme of my *A Common Law: The Law of Nations and Western Civilization*.

ECONOMICS

In the last chapter, we sketched the outline of "State of Nature Politics." We will now do the same here, and explore "State of Nature Economics." For there exists an economic counterpart to natural rights theory, and it is saddled with the same core problem-set. It seeks a reality behind the supposed façade of convention, of civil society, private law, and sovereignty, in the same way that natural rights doctrine seeks to dissociate life, liberty, and property from civil authority.

Adam Smith's Physiocratic Economics

As nature provided the framework for law, it provided the framework for economics. The new approach went by the name *physiocracy,* which, tellingly enough, means "rule by nature." Adam Smith harnessed the physiocratic framework in his epoch-making work, *An Inquiry into the Nature and Causes of the Wealth of Nations.* [27] Smith sought to counter the influence of mercantilist thought which to that point had dominated public opinion and government policy.

Smith's target was the ostensible mercantilist equation of wealth and money. He described mercantilism as the pursuit of national wealth by the accumulation of money in the form of bullion. To this end, gold and silver exportation was to be restricted and a favorable balance of trade pursued, thus keeping gold and silver in-country.

---

[27] The treatment which best brings this out in Smith's economics is Stadermann and Steiger, *Schulökonomik* [Schools of Economic Thought]. By the way, is it entirely coincidental that *The Wealth of Nations* was published in the same year, 1776, as the Declaration of Independence?

Smith disputed this equation of wealth and money. His view was that the wealth of nations consisted not in money but in actual productive capacity, the ability to generate goods and services. His goal was to establish the primacy of free trade as a principle of international relations, but in order to do so he delivered a hostage to fortune. For, like the natural-rights theorists who sought to refound rights and liberties on a basis beyond convention, Smith sought to refound free trade on the state of nature. As we shall see, this would yield a baneful harvest.

Using this theoretical basis, Smith posited false dichotomies which at best confuse the issue. Firstly, in order to combat the alleged mercantilist position favoring the producer over the consumer, he asserted the primacy of consumption over production.

> Consumption is the sole end and purpose of all production; and the interest of the producer ought to be attended to only so far as it may be necessary for promoting that of the consumer. The maxim is so perfectly self-evident that it would be absurd to attempt to prove it. But in the mercantile system the interest of the consumer is almost constantly sacrificed to that of the producer; and it seems to consider production, and not consumption, as the ultimate end and object of all industry and commerce.[28]

But the whole notion of favoring one of these over the other is chimerical. For consumption and production are two sides of the same relation, and they each depend equally on the other: one cannot consume without first producing (or someone producing for him). Jean-Baptiste Say expressed the idea succinctly in what is known as Say's Law: supply creates its own demand. Which is to say, supply, or production, and demand, or consumption, are two sides

---

[28] Smith, *An Inquiry into the Nature and Causes of the Wealth of Nations,* Book IV, ch. 8, para. 49.

of one and the same equation.

This truncation has beset economics ever since. It has led to the focus on distribution, and the efficiency thereof through the market process, while relegating production to the status of "production function," as a sort of black box, taken for granted. Smith's emphasis on the division of labor being limited by the extent of the market is an expression of this fixation. The size of the market certainly is an important aspect, but only one aspect, in determining the division of labor.

One false dichotomy leads to another, to wit, Smith's definition of wealth in which he opposes money to goods. Here, Smith is attacking the equation of wealth and money, to which he opposes productive labor resulting in goods as the true content of a nation's wealth.

The real price of every thing, what every thing really costs to the man who wants to acquire it, is the toil and trouble of acquiring it. What every thing is really worth to the man who has acquired it, and who wants to dispose of it or exchange it for something else, is the toil and trouble which it can save to himself, and which it can impose upon other people. What is bought with money or with goods is purchased by labour, as much as what we acquire by the toil of our own body. That money or those goods indeed save us this toil. They contain the value of a certain quantity of labour which we exchange for what is supposed at the time to contain the value of an equal quantity. *Labour was the first price, the original purchase-money that was paid for all things.* It was not by gold or by silver, but by labour, that all the wealth of the world was originally purchased; and its value, to those who possess it, and who want to exchange it for some new productions, is precisely equal to the quantity of labour which it can enable them to purchase or command.[29]

Money is merely representative of the underlying reality, which in Smith's view is the labor expended in the production process. Labor is the source of the value we attribute to marketable goods, and wealth is the sum total of such goods.

Smith here followed John Locke, who, as we have seen, attributed the origin of property to labor. Locke did so because labor supposedly was the ultimate source of economic value.

> ...[S]upposing the world given, as it was, to the children of men in common, we see how labour could make men distinct titles to several parcels of it, for their private uses; wherein there could be no doubt of right, no room for quarrel.
>
> Nor is it so strange, as perhaps before consideration it may appear, that the property of labour should be able to over-balance the community of land: for it is labour indeed that put the difference of value on every thing....[30]

Here Smith simply adapted the Lockean state of nature understanding of civil society to economics. Money is something added to the economic process in order to facilitate it, but it is by no means essential to it: barter could just as well take place, albeit certainly with attendant inconvenience.

Excepting Say, the labor theory of value was shared by all the classical economists including Marx, who in fact derived his critique of capitalism precisely by assuming it. Essentially, since labor is the source of all value, capitalists in their accumulation of profit

---

[29] Smith, *An Inquiry into the Nature and Causes of the Wealth of Nations,* Book I, ch. 5, para. 2. Emphasis added.

[30] Locke, *Two Treatises of Government,* "Of Civil Government," vol. II, chap. v, §§. 39–40.

were appropriating surplus value which by right accrued to the laborers. Marxism would eliminate this inequity by eliminating the capitalist, so creating the workers' paradise.

From Classical to Neoclassical Economics

In response, a new school of economic thought arose, the so-called neoclassical school, which while sharing Smith's conviction of the importance of free trade to the wealth of nations, parted ways with him with regard to the doctrine of economic value.

The neoclassicists substituted the principle of marginal utility for that of labor as the basis of economic value. That is, they exchanged the objective approach, in which value is considered to inhere in labor, for the subjective approach, in which the appraisal of economic actors is made the source of value. "The meaning goods have for us, which we call value, is merely transferred. Originally, only need-satisfactions have a meaning for us, in that the maintenance of our life and our welfare depends on them; as a logical consequence, however, we transfer this meaning to those goods the disposition over which we are conscious of being dependent upon for the satisfaction of these needs."[31] Value is rooted in the relative satisfaction – the marginal utility – a good provides, not in the labor used to produce that good.

But that is as far as they got. Neoclassicists too shared Smith's conviction regarding the primacy of consumption and efficient distribution via the market as the subject matter of economics. For them as well, money was a superfluous albeit useful addendum; true

---

[31] Menger, *Principles of Economics,* ch. 3, §. 2b, p. 107. The translation is mine, from the original German text. The Dingwall/Hoselitz translation (James Dingwall and Bert F. Hoselitz, trans., *Principles of Economics,* New York: The Free Press, 1950; online edition, The Mises Institute, 2004) is too imprecise to be of use here.

economic science involved getting behind the "veil of money" to the real substrate of concrete goods.

This agenda became explicit in the work of Eugen von Böhm-Bawerk, one of the founders of the neoclassical "Austrian" school of economics. Böhm-Bawerk is interesting in that he penetrated to the very core of the issue, only decisively to turn aside from the appropriate course in order to remain faithful to state of nature economics.

Goods versus Rights as the Focus of Economics

The motivation behind Böhm's investigation was righteous indignation. Economists had been smuggling a new category into the ranks of economic goods, namely "rights and relations" (German: Rechte und Verhältnisse), reflecting the veritable asset explosion of multiplying forms of credit and goodwill, forms which appeared to have increased the total wealth exponentially.

The chief instigator of this revolution in economics was the Scot Henry Dunning Macleod. Drawing upon his experience in the real world of banking and finance, Macleod had come to the conclusion that it was not material goods at all that constituted the subject matter of economics, but the rights to those goods. "As Jurisprudence is the Science which treats exclusively about Rights, and not about Things, so **Economics** is the Science which treats exclusively about the **Exchanges** of **Rights**, and not the **Exchanges** of **Things**."[32] The Western system of private law had led to the multiplication of forms of rights, each exchangeable, each with monetary value in its own right; and for Macleod it was absurd that economists continued to ignore the existence thereof.

---

[32] *The Elements of Economics,* v. I, p. 151. Macleod was a great believer in highlighting via boldface print.

Now the question at issue is no trifling one. The property afloat in this country in bills of exchange, bank notes, and bank credits alone, is upwards of £600,000,000, and the question is, Whether this is a real and independent value, or only a myth? All Political Economists, from the days of Turgot, maintain that it is nothing, a mere nonentity, that it is of no more value than the paper it is written on. We, on the contrary, maintain in opposition to the entire body of writers in France and England, from Turgot to Mr. John S. Mill, that it is a real value, that is a separate and independent value over and above, and perfectly distinct from money or commodities, and we have the most perfect conviction that we are right.[33]

Macleod was aware that the criticism of his view centered on the charge of double-counting, of asserting the existence of an economic good on the one hand and a separate right to that same good, an IOU of one form or another, as being itself likewise an economic good. Böhm-Bawerk expressed the objection this way: "One may summarize the conditions upon which Macleod's doctrine is based in the following two statements: 1) When A lends a dollar to B, B possesses in this dollar a corporeal good valued at one dollar. 2) In the right of obligation to the return of the dollar lent, A possesses an immaterial good with a present value likewise approaching a dollar, and which is not identical to the material dollar."[34] If this is true, says Böhm, then indeed, "credit creates new, previously non-existent goods, and the goods-doubling power of credit would truly be

---

[33] *Elements of Political Economy,* pp. 325–326.
[34] *Rechte und Verhältnisse,* p. 11. Again, the translation is mine; the Huncke translation ("Whether Legal Rights and Relationships are Economic Goods") is imprecise.

a miraculous fact, albeit still a fact."[35] But this cannot be; for it is to count the economic good and the right, of which the economic good is an object, as two separate goods. "Today there can be no doubt that the chief principle [der Hauptsatz] of this doctrine is erroneous [ein Irrsatz]: the double-counting made here with the credited object and the right directed to this object, or made with obligation and debt, is all too obvious."[36]

Back in 1858, in his *Elements of Political Economy*, Macleod had already retorted to criticism similar to that made by Böhm in 1881:

> Now, who can deny that the present value of a debt, payable at some future period, is a separate and independent value? It is a marketable commodity, it may be bought and sold like a pound of sugar, and the money that is paid for it does not represent it any more than the money represents any commodity that is exchanged for it.... Now, what is a Bill of Exchange? It is nothing but a debt payable three months after date, say; and that debt has a present and separate value, quite independent of the money that will ultimately pay it. Now, when we affirm that credit is capital, we mean nothing more than this, that operations take place where one or both sides of the transaction are debts. That sales of goods and services occur, where a "promise to pay" forms one side of the transaction. A proposition, we presume, which no one in his senses will deny. We make no assertion involving the stupid blunder that the same thing can be in two places at once.[37]

Apparently, Böhm (and others) had been misreading Macleod, asserting that he counted both the economic good and the right

---

[35] *Rechte und Verhältnisse*, p. 11.

[36] *Rechte und Verhältnisse*, p. 10.

[37] *Elements of Political Economy*, p. 325.

attached to that good as two separate economic goods. This is not what he was doing; rather, he was consistently making the attempt at replacing "goods" with "rights" as the material of exchange and thus of economics.

But Macleod's language sometimes added to the confusion. For example, in the *Elements of Economics*[38] he writes "*On the* **Three Species** *of Wealth or of* Economic Quantities." These comprise, firstly, "**Material** or **Corporeal Things**... such as lands, houses, money, corn, timber, cattle, and herds of all sorts, jewelry, minerals, and innumerable things of this nature which can be bought and sold, and whose Value is measured in money." Then comes "**Immaterial Wealth**," including personal services ("A person may sell his Labour or Services in many capacities for money, such as a ploughman, an artisan, a carpenter, or as a physician, an advocate, an engineer, an actor, or a soldier: and when he receives a definite sum of money for such Labour or Service its *Value is measured in money*, as precisely as if it were a material chattel" – thus, Adam Smith's labor, Say's immaterial products of labor and services, Senior's knowledge. Thirdly, "**Incorporeal Wealth**," consisting in "vast masses of Property which exist only in the form of abstract Rights, quite separate and severed from any material substances, which can all be bought and sold, and whose *Value can be measured in money*, exactly like that of any material chattel." Therefore there are "**three** distinct Orders of Quantities which can be bought and sold, or exchanged: and therefore which satisfy the definition of Wealth."

Here Macleod lines up things, services, and rights as three different forms of wealth, instead of being clear that all three categories are forms of rights.

The confusion becomes complete when he enumerates the forms of exchange that may take place:

---

[38] *Elements of Economics,* pp. 138–140.

1. The exchange of a Material thing for a Material thing.— Such as so much corn, cattle, or land for so much gold.

2. The exchange of a Material thing for Labour or a Service.— As when gold or silver money is given as wages, fees, or salary for services done.

3. The exchange of a Material thing for a Right—as when gold money is given in exchange for the funds, or a Copyright, or Bill of Exchange.

4. The exchange of Labour for Labour—as when persons agree to exchange one kind of Labour for another kind of Labour.

5. The exchange of Labour for a Right—as when wages or salaries are paid in bank notes.

6. The exchange of one Right for another Right—as when a Banker buys a Bill of exchange, which is a Right, by giving in exchange for it a Credit in his books, which is another Right.[39]

This is inexcusable. For in the same book, only ten pages further down, Macleod states, as quoted above (p. 34), that it is rights, not things, which are exchanged, and which can be divided into three categories corresponding exactly with the aforementioned list: "**Corporeal** or **Material** **Property** or **Rights**," then "**Immaterial** **Property** [or rights]," lastly "**Incorporeal Property** [or rights]."[40]

The confusion of putting rights and objects of rights on a line is what led Böhm-Bawerk to launch his criticism. It was not Macleod who fell into his error, though, but others who, while professing to see the error of Macleod's ways, nevertheless persisted in their own.[41] For his part, Böhm resolutely stuck with the Smithian

---

[39] *Elements of Economics,* p. 141.

[40] *Elements of Economics,* pp. 151–152.

[41] cf. Böhm-Bawerk, "Whether Legal Rights and Relationships are Economic Goods," pp. 37f.

doctrine of goods broadly understood as the products of labor – material things and personal services – as the substance of exchange, rejecting Macleod's rights-based approach absolutely.

For this reason Böhm failed in his attempt to develop a satisfactory theory of interest, to which he devoted two massive volumes. He simply could not come up with an original rationale for, as Aristotle put it, money begetting money, and was forced to make interest a derivative concept, with profit-generating capital goods – for him, the true underlying reality – somehow being the source of it.[42]

Since then, neoclassical economics as a whole has failed to come up with a satisfactory theory explaining either money or interest. This is due to its principled decision to view goods as the proper subject matter of economics, while consigning money, indeed the entire sphere of "incorporeal property," to a derivative category, nonessential to theory.

Keynes was aware of the problem, and in his own way set out to fix it: by turning it on its head. Instead of goods being original and money derivative, he made money to be original and goods to be derivative. Money, which could be created ex nihilo by the government (truly a godlike entity in this regard) could of itself generate productive capacity. Keynes thus advanced a proposition reversing Say's Law: to wit, demand creates its own supply.

The reality which Macleod perceived was that the universe of rights transforms and multiplies wealth.[43] The material substrate of

---

[42] For a detailed critique of Böhm-Bawerk's approach, and a thorough examination of rights versus goods as the subject matter of economics, see Appendix 2: Rights and Economics.

[43] This is also the subject of Hernando de Soto's important books, *The Other Path* and *The Mystery of Capital*. For a distillation of De Soto's thesis, see my *Investing in the New Normal,* ch. 2, "Lifting the Bell Jar."

wealth is not the same thing as wealth, and without the panoply of rights through which the material substrate is mediated in an economy, that material substrate is left unproductive, at a subsistence level, at least for the mass of men. This is why tribal and feudal societies anciently, and socialist societies in modern times, never have gotten much farther than a minimal level of productivity.

From Possession- to Property-Based Economics

The reality of the situation is that property is not "just there," it is a quality attaching to things *only within the legal context*, the context of private law. Gunnar Heinsohn (sociologist) and Otto Steiger (economist) make this clear in their application of the *distinction between possession and property*.[44] This legal distinction is unavailable to economists who are unaware of, or who refuse to recognize, the fundamental importance of the legal sphere to economics. Possession concerns goods and services – actual use – while property concerns the invisible layer of titles and obligations applied over those goods and services, engendered by the human will, which is capable of *obligating to future performances*.

> Obligation serves a dual purpose, that of meeting needs for which things are not appropriate (services, works) but beyond that *securing for the future things themselves, by means of the human will*. The significance of obligation is not so much to make possible services or the communication of things – this can be achieved by mere

---

[44] First explained in *Eigentum, Zins und Geld: Ungelöste Rätsel der Wirtschaftswissenschaft* [Property, Interest, and Money: Unsolved Mysteries of Economic Science], fourth, revised edition. Marburg: Metropolis Verlag, 2006. For English-language treatments, see "Property Titles as the Clue to a Successful Transformation" and "The Property Theory of Interest and Money."

factual performance – but much rather *that security of the future exist*, partly by making possible a present performance or communication without damage and hazard, and partly through which the future possession of an object is secured in a manner often not afforded even by continuous possession.[45]

This distinction is what Marx and others were groping after in their distinction between use value and exchange value. The distinction pertains to the internal and the external dimensions, respectively, of the formations comprising society. Use – the possession dimension – is group-internal, while obligation – the property dimension – is group-external. As such, the distinction is fundamental. The one involves the exploitation of the good or service; the other, the capacity, as it were, to exploit the exploitation, by means of pledge upon which credit is based, above and beyond the exploitation of the good.

Economically, therefore, property is the result when potential obligation is added to possession (possession + potential obligation = property), potential obligation being the capacity to promise, which in turn leads to the capacity to burden, to encumber, to collateralize property, which enables the receipt of credit while retaining possession, and thus use, of the property involved. All other functions of property are already contained in possession. Therefore, in the property regime the object of property can be retained, and so exploited, while also collateralized for credit. This "having one's cake and eating it too" is what enabled the explosion of wealth lauded by Macleod and was so inexplicable to Böhm-Bawerk – whose response, in principle, was of the same ilk as Aristotle's was to the idea of interest.

To account for this phenomenon, Heinsohn and Steiger

---

[45] Stahl, *Private Law,* p. 95. Emphasis added.

developed a new concept: *property premium*. Property premium is "... a non-physical yield of security which accrues from property as long as it is unencumbered and not economically activated. The premium allows proprietors to enter credit contracts, and is a measure of the potential of individuals to become creditors and debtors."[46] It is the "potential obligation" in the equation just put forward. The establishment of a regime of secured possession, of ownership against all the world, enabled by the umbrella of sovereignty and the instrumentality of private law, generates this property premium, this "non-physical yield of security."

The property owner puts property premium to use by encumbering his property in exchange for money (legal tender[47]). And so we arrive at the cornerstone of the regime of property. The system runs on credit and debt; this is done through agreements establishing those credit-debt relations; these agreement establish obligations which are finally settled; such settlement is realized through the institution of money. Money therefore is anything but adventitious. Without it, economic activity cannot advance much beyond the most primitive stage.

In the modern financial system, money is created precisely by actualizing the property premium, through credit/debt relations

---

[46] Heinsohn and Steiger, "The Property Theory of Interest and Money," in *What Is Money?*, p. 82.

[47] "Legal tender is anything recognized by law as a means to settle a public or private debt or meet a financial obligation, including tax payments, contracts, and legal fines or damages. The national currency is legal tender in practically every country. A creditor is legally obligated to accept legal tender toward repayment of a debt." *Investopedia*, https://www.investopedia.com/terms/l/legal-tender.asp.

between borrowers and banks.[48] Banks are simply those institutions in society vested with the authority, granted either by custom or legislation, to make this conversion. The transaction accomplishing this, stripped down to its bare essentials, is as follows: a property owner wishes to obtain the means for carrying out transactions. He does so without relinquishing his property, for the bank has no desire to buy it – it only wishes to earn the interest it can gain on the loan. Because of this, the property-owning borrower can "have his cake and eat it too": he borrows from a bank legal tender – the currency of the realm – and he does so at the expense, not of his property, but of the pledge of his property, surety in case he does not repay the amount he borrows. The bank issues this medium of transactions, this money, to some percentage of the value of the surety, i.e., of the collateral put up by the borrower. Hence, what this money represents is the value, not of the property of the issuer, but of the borrower. And this yields a conclusion of the highest importance, simple though it sounds: since money represents the value of the security, its backing is the collateral.

This also explains the origin of interest. When, e.g., landed property is mortgaged, the bank converts the property of the owner into a circulating medium, and takes over the property premium from the landowner. For the landowner, then, property premium is the means to obtain circulating medium; for the bank, it is transformed into interest.[49]

---

[48] There have been various "money methods" used in history. Coinage is one; most-marketable commodities is another. Our modern system of money is based on the banking system. For more on this, see my *Follow the Money* as well as Joseph Schumpeter, *Treatise on Money* (Aalten: Word-Bridge Publishing, 2014).

[49] For some inexplicable reason, Heinsohn and Steiger envisage money as

The Achievement of James Steuart

Yet another Scot, James Steuart, originally pioneered this understanding of money. Steuart made the astute observation that interest derived from the advantage of circulation. Where this advantage is lacking, so is the rationale for borrowing. [50] But where bank money is accepted as circulating medium, as legal tender, its advantages over metallic currencies become plain. It was Steuart who first satisfactorily explained this situation.

Steuart is the "forgotten man" among 18th-century economists – forgotten because he was eclipsed by Adam Smith, whose *Wealth of Nations* enshrined the commodity view of money.[51] Only in our day is his work being rediscovered, it being the simplest and best explanation of the workings of money, credit, and banking. Through the examination of actual bank practice in his day – apparently something beneath the dignity of true economists – Steuart uncovered the principles which underlie the creation of money in a banking system. These principles had been developed and applied in practice, without recourse to theory. (Theory, in this matter

---

representing the value of the property of the *issuer* rather than the borrower, with interest being compensation for the resulting sacrifice of their property premium. This mars their otherwise highly fertile thesis.

[50] "And for what does he pay... interest? Not because he has gratuitously received any value from the bank, since in his obligation he has given a full equivalent for the notes; but the obligation he has given carries interest, and the notes carry none. Why? Because the one circulates like money, the other does not. For this advantage, therefore, of circulation, not for any additional value, does the landed man pay interest to the bank." Sir James Steuart, *An Inquiry into the Principles of Political Economy*, Book IV, Part I, ch. 7.

[51] Stadermann and Steiger, *Schulökonomik*, contains the best treatment of Steuart's economics.

perhaps more than any other, has left practice to fend for itself.)

Steuart drew his primary example from the practice of Scottish banks, specifically banks of circulation upon private credit (i.e., mortgage),[52] which in his day had proved unusually successful in spurring economic growth and development. Such banks were formed by associations of "men of property," each of whom contributed to form the original stock, something "consisting indifferently of any species of property... engaged to all the creditors of the company, as a security for the notes they propose to issue." This original stock is *not the money base;* it is not the basis upon which banknotes are issued. Rather, it is merely a guarantee of the good faith of the company. It is "a pledge, as it were, for the faithful discharge of the trust reposed in the bank: without such a pledge, the public could have no security to indemnify it, in case the bank should issue notes for no permanent value received." Therefore, "large bank stocks ... serve only to establish their credit; to secure the confidence of the public, who cannot see into their administration; but who willingly believe, that men who have considerable property pledged in security of their good faith, will not probably deceive them."

What, then, is the money base? Not the bank's own property, reserves, holdings, or stock; *it is the securities given in exchange for loans.* "So soon as confidence is established with the public, they grant credits, or cash accompts, upon good security; concerning which they make the proper regulations." In this manner the bank, using a metaphor near and dear to Steuart's heart, melts down solid property into "symbolical," paper money.[53]

---

[52] Steuart, *An Inquiry into the Principles of Political Economy*, Book IV, Part II, ch. 4. This chapter contains the definitive statement in this regard. Unless otherwise noted, the following quotations come from it.

[53] "The ruling principle in private credit, and the basis on which it rests, is

This form of credit, called "private credit" by Steuart and consisting of credit against personal property such as land and homes, is considered by him the most reliable form. Mercantile (commercial) credit, on the other hand, being loans issued against the prospects of business enterprise, is less reliable and therefore subject to a higher interest rate. Thus, banks established upon private credit are sounder than those established upon mercantile credit.[54] The form of security required by the bank, in exchange for which the bank lends, determines the quality of currency it issues. "Which way ... can the public judge of the affairs of bankers, except by attending to the nature of the securities upon which they give credit"?[55]

The bank maintains a certain level of reserves, which in Steuart's day were coin – for the notes issued were in principle repayable in coin – in order to make repayments and to serve as a buffer for bad loans. "Nothing but experience can enable them to determine the proportion between the coin to be kept in their coffers, and the paper in circulation. This proportion varies even according to circumstances." It is therefore but a percentage of the total outstanding loans. And it need be only that.

---

the facility of converting, into money, the effects of the debtor; because the capital and interest are constantly supposed to be demandable. The proper way, therefore, to support this sort of credit to the utmost, is to contrive a ready method of appretiating every subject affectable by debts; and secondly, of melting it down into symbolical or paper money." Steuart, *An Inquiry into the Principles of Political Economy*, Book IV, Part II, ch. 2.

[54] Oddly enough, English banking adopted the opposite approach: mercantile credit was preferred.

[55] Steuart, *An Inquiry into the Principles of Political Economy*, Book IV, Part II, ch. 5.

To drive his point home, Steuart uses the example of "an honest man, intelligent, and capable to undertake a bank."

> I say that such a person, without one shilling of stock, may carry on a bank of domestic circulation, to as good purpose as if he had a million; and his paper will be every bit as good as that of the bank of England. Every note he issues will be secured on good private security; this security carries interest to him, in proportion to the money which has been advanced by him, and stands good for the notes he has issued. Suppose then that after having issued for a million sterling, all the notes should return upon him in one day. Is it not plain, that they will find, with the honest banker, the original securities, taken by him at the time he issued them; and is it not true, that he will have, belonging to himself, the interest received upon these securities, while his notes were in circulation, except so far as this interest has been spent in carrying on the business of his bank?

To minds steeped in the notion that money is the most marketable commodity, such a statement is astounding. And yet, it makes perfect sense. If money is issued against good security, it represents that security. It does not represent the bank's property, but the borrower's.

This is the core of the property regime, and the engine of economic growth. "The metamorphosis of property premium into a charge of interest owed by a debtor in every credit contract is at the root of capitalism's envied *accumulation* and *technical progress* in the same manner as the non-metamorphosis is at the root of its deplorable *crises*."[56]

---

[56] Heinsohn and Steiger, "Property Titles as the Clue to a Successful Transformation," in *Verpflichtungsökonomik,* p. 210.

Common-Law Economic Valuation[57]

Valuation as a market function is part and parcel of this same money-issuing, credit-generating process. Valuation is not first attained through the process of buying and selling, but through the process of encumbering and collateralizing property to issue money in credit contracts. This is because credit contracts, not sales contracts, are original; sales contracts follow after.

> Property titles are always transferred in creditor-debtor contracts in which both creditor and debtor are proprietors. These contracts are divided into mere *credit contracts* and *sales contracts*. In the former, claims to property are transferred but not claims to possession, rights to the physical use of goods or resources. In the latter, claims to property are transferred *uno actu* with claims to possession. Sales contracts are always subordinated to the credit contracts whose fulfilment they serve.[58]

The issue itself forms the original valuation, money being issued in terms of the value of the collateral. The property put up as collateral receives its valuation in the credit contract through which money is obtained.

Valuation being inherent in the issue of money, it is not dependent on the previous valuation of any commodity but instead is the source of the valuation of commodities. Contemporary goods-based economic theory, viewing money as the most marketable commodity, usually views the precious metals, preeminently gold, as the standard by which to value everything else. But this is to put the cart before the horse; and viewed from this angle it is easy to

---

[57] For legal valuation, see pp. 124ff.

[58] Heinsohn and Steiger, "The Property Theory of Interest and Money," in *What Is Money?*, p. 82.

understand Stadermann and Steiger's impatience:

> Hundreds of years of "value theory" tradition make it difficult to understand that investigation into the origin of the value of economic goods is not a scientific question. Economic science has difficulty divesting itself of that medieval insistence on investigating the *substance* of things in order, in the manner of natural science since the Enlightenment, to pass over to investigating the *relations* between economic phenomena. For this it requires no classical or neoclassical value mysticism. The value of economic goods is measured in differentiable money units in no other way than temperature is in various degree scales. Establishing a currency unit is an act just like establishing the Celsius scale for the measurement of temperature. Why the temperature difference between two aggregate conditions of water is divisible in one hundred equal intervals cannot be answered scientifically. Not only three but a thousand, yea innumerable foundations were possible for measuring temperature; it is only convention that made use of the decimal system of 100 sections for the scale.[59]

The value of things is not inherent in certain things which then serve as the basis for the valuation of everything else. It is not a characteristic to be discovered by peeling away convention to get to the original, "natural" state. Valuation is a matter precisely of convention and agreement: it is an affair of common-law functionality.

To summarize, credit and debt is be the stuff of economic activity at its most basic level, with exchange of goods and services erected atop that basis. The common law provides the forms and institutions enabling expanding economic activity. Economic activity is conducted using the rights and jural relations the common law

---

[59] Stadermann and Steiger, *Schulökonomik*, p. 15.

provides. This invisible web of commitments is what enables the co-operative activity of myriads of disparate individuals and associations to join together to form a dynamic economy. These legal institutions are made possible by the umbrella of sovereignty.

As such, state of nature economics, like state of nature politics, is a fairy tale devised after the fact, to help legitimize a "natural" social order – in fact, a de-confessionalized social order.

The common-law economy did not arise in a vacuum. Like constitutionalism, it arose within the context of Christian nationhood and sovereignty. It is the fruit of Christian-historical civilization. And therefore of confessional Christianity. Of course, the state of nature paradigm could not allow such a raison d'être to stand. Its alternative was state of nature religion, to which we now turn.

RELIGION

As noted earlier, the founder of state of nature politics, Hugo Grotius, was motivated by the desire to move beyond confessional religion, specifically Christianity of one form or another, as the basis for legitimating sovereignty. Sovereignty had to be grounded in something other than divine right and a common religious confession, and he felt he had found that grounding in the institutions of private law: property and contract. These could serve as institutions not merely serving society, but creating society.

Natural Religion – the Legitimating Ideology

Of course, these pillars required a form of religious window-dressing, and this came in the form of what came to be known as natural religion, which we call state of nature religion – religion elevated above differences of doctrine, a creed rejecting creedalism, a universal faith uniting all without divisive and contentious criteria.

Grotius himself was a pioneer of this natural religion. He viewed biblical revelation as restricted to the Jews and the Christians, and instead of embracing the distinctives it entailed, emphasized certain universal principles in accordance with nonsectarian natural law, which everyone might accept.[60] And the Enlightenment followed

---

[60] For example, "Grotius ... combines rabbinical teaching with the New Testament to give a clearly dispensational interpretation of the place of biblical law.... By affirming that the law as given to the Gentiles after the Noahic flood is the only law from the Old Testament that is binding on them, Grotius is incorporating a Talmudic, rabbinical teaching which emphasized Old Testament law as the exclusive property of the Jews." *The Debate that Changed the West*, pp. 71–72.

him in this, advocating latitudinarianism in the church and the disestablishment of Christianity in favor of non-judgmental, non-dogmatic civil religion in the political realm.[61] So, in the Declaration of Independence we end up with a bare reference to "the Creator" endowing us with rights in the Grotian manner, God being necessary to underwrite the system.[62]

This would have momentous consequences on the social order. To understand this, we need to take another look at Grotius' manipulation of the doctrine of subjective right.

The Transformation of Subjective Right

This doctrine entails a specific conception of human nature, viz., one in which human being are seen as autonomous actors, and as centers of judicial spheres of influence from which their worlds are ordered (see the discussion on pp. 10ff. above).

However, the doctrine of subjective right, as Stahl rightly noted, is only a secondary principle of legal formation. It is subordinate to the primary principle of objective law. But Grotius and his followers, including John Locke, turned this hierarchy on its head, making the objective legal order the consequence of subjective right.

By making this secondary principle into the primary overarching principle of law and order, and in fact the source of sovereignty, the natural-rights philosophers in fact reversed one of the pillars of Christian civilization: the understanding that man was fallen, and that the institutions of society did not derive from him but were instituted over and around him, to hedge him in, as it were; in so doing to provide, in order and in authority, the basis for a sound,

---

[61] An excellent overview of this process is to be found in Henning Graf Reventlow, *The Authority of the Bible and the Rise of the Modern World* (Philadelphia: Fortress Press, 1985).

[62] See p. 9 above.

healthy, viable liberty.

The Pelagian Result: Natural Rights

Hence the Augustinian view of the depravity of human nature was tossed overboard in favor of the optimistic view thereof,[63] wherein man, if not perfectible (although for many the perfectibility of man became a popular corollary), at least was capable of establishing proper institutions by his own device, by consulting his own nature. The state of nature was not distinguished by being corrupt, but by being sub-optimal; man came together in society voluntarily – society is not pre-existing – and he did so, according to Grotius, because of a "drive toward sociability," a need for companionship and for the benefits of cooperation. And things did not stop there. "When, however, Thomasius replaced the drive toward sociability with the *drive toward happiness*, by which the individual of necessity becomes isolated, the last remnant of an objective legal principle was eliminated."[64]

As a result, natural-rights philosophy gave birth to the atomistic individual as the source of authority, sovereignty, and law. The 18th century was an arid age for associationalism, as all of its political theories were individualistic and contractual, leaving no room for an articulated associational life.[65] Every form of association became voluntary, and the family, the church, the state, the nation, all of which assume participation prior to consent, had to be contorted

---

[63] Both Grotius and Locke dissented from the Augustinian doctrine of original sin.

[64] Stahl, *Principles of Law,* p. 27. The pursuit of happiness, which eliminates any objective legal principle, in the Declaration of Independence becomes the source of law!

[65] For details see Otto von Gierke, *Natural Law and the Theory of Society 1500–1800.*

into conformity with this doctrine. There was no room in this philosophy for pre-existing authority.

From Classical to Progressive Liberalism

The counterpart to this focus on subjective right as the source of
authority and law was a truncated notion of justice. Now the common law – this universal, integrating law – is itself the expression of
strict justice. Grotius saw this clearly in describing strict justice as
the justice involved in property and obligation – Aristotle's commutative justice. By contrast, he categorized distributive justice as justice in the broad sense, because it was not amenable to enforcement
by civil (private) law. As such, it was not even justice at all, but mere
(unenforceable) morality.

Now Grotius was indeed on to something here. The distinction
between the strict justice expressed in civil private law and the
"broad" justice which is distributive justice is an eminently valid
one. Properly understood, this distinction establishes the difference
between common law, or external (civil) private law, and the internal law of each individual organization or association, for the latter
is governed precisely by this other principle, the principle of distributive justice. But Grotius' achievement was vitiated by the fatal decision to eliminate distributive justice from any consideration in
law, thus destroying the notion of pre-existing authority structures
with internal law-spheres that need to be recognized as such.

Distributive justice did not stay down; it would return, but by
the back door, as it were, to engage the hamstrung common law in
mortal combat.

This "back door" was what came to be known as the social question. The focus on property and contract as the be-all-and-end-all
of social order is the basis of what was then known as "Whiggery"
and is now known as classical liberalism. This entailed an apotheosis
of property and contract (contractualism), turning them into

absolute values around which the remainder of the social order was arranged. It led to the sort of social order memorialized by Charles Dickens. For not only did the law prioritize property, but there was no longer the counterbalancing force in the public square which the church had provided with her ministry of mercy. Classical liberalism eliminated the public church and put all the emphasis on property. The result indeed was "Hard Times" – the title of a famous Dickens novel.[66]

This called forth a backlash in which property itself came under scrutiny as being the problem rather than the solution. Such already had become clear during the period of the French Revolution, when François-Noël Babeuf led his conspiracy to replace the Directory with a regime installing common property. It was also the driving force behind William Godwin's *Enquiry Concerning Political Justice* (first edition 1793) proclaiming the perfectibility of man precisely through the elimination of institutions such as property. And behind all of this, of course, loomed Jean-Jacques Rousseau ("The first man who enclosed a plot of ground and thought of saying, 'This is mine,' and found others stupid enough to believe him, was the true founder of civil society"[67]).

Taking its cue from Adam Smith and his emphasis on consumption over production, the social question focused not on the creation of wealth but its distribution. The fact that this distribution was unequal was evident to all; and that this unequal distribution was likewise inequitable, was the conviction of many. Thanks to the deemphasis on the church and her teaching regarding the depravity of man, the conviction that human misery might have some link to such depravity was deprecated. Another root of the problem had to

---

[66] The gold standard put the icing on the cake. For an extended exposition, see my *Follow the Money,* ch. 13, "The Social Question Unraveled."

[67] Rousseau, *Discourse on Inequality*, p. 60.

be discovered; and it was promptly found in property and the other institutions of civil society. Godwin, for example, attributed "almost all the vices and misery that are seen in civil society to human institutions. Political regulations, and the established administration of property, are with him the fruitful sources of all evil, the hotbeds of all the crimes that degrade mankind."[68]

In true dialectical fashion, the classical liberal apotheosis of property generated its obverse, the vilification of property.

At the root of this development was precisely confusion – willful confusion – regarding the nature of justice. Thomas Chalmers was one of the first to point out what would go wrong when charity was converted into a matter of entitlement. "We have long thought that by a legal provision for indigence, two principles of our moral nature have been confounded, which are radically distinct from each other.... These two principles are humanity and justice, whereof the latter is the only proper object of legislation – which, by attempting the enforcement of the former, has overstepped altogether its own rightful boundaries."[69]

This confusion of justice and mercy led to the situation in which the alleviation of poverty is to be accomplished not through charity and self-help backed by the public church's ministry of mercy, but as a matter of right whereby one simply may claim the shortfall from his neighbor.

> Whatever the calls be, which the poverty of a human being may have on the compassion of his fellows – it has no claims whatever upon their justice. The confusion of these two virtues in the ethical system will tend to actual confusion and disorder, when introduced in the laws and administrations of human society. The

---

[68] Malthus, *An Essay on the Principle of Population,* chap. 10, paragraph 4.
[69] *Problems of Poverty,* p. 201.

proper remedy, or remedy of nature, for the wretchedness of the few, is the kindness of the many. But when the heterogeneous imagination of a right is introduced in to this department of human affairs, and the imagination is sanctioned by the laws of the country, then one of two things must follow – Either an indefinite encroachment on property, so as ultimately to reduce to a sort of agrarian level of all the families of the land; or, if to postpone this consequence a rigid dispensation be adopted, the disappointment of a people who have been taught to feel themselves aggrieved, the innumerable heart-burnings which law itself has conjured up, and no administration of that law, however skilful, can appease.[70]

A prophetic statement indeed! And it leads to the inevitable conclusion: "Pauperism in so far as sustained on the principle that each man, simply because he exists, holds a right on other men or on society for existence, is a thing not to be regulated but destroyed."[71]

This confusion was made possible by the very natural-rights paradigm that was supposed to solve our problems by superseding narrow confessional politics. Grotius delivered his hostage to fortune when he eliminated distributive justice from consideration in law. This made subjective right into the source of law and social order; it made the individual primary; but in principle it also eliminated the associations and institutions in society which relied not on consent but on pre-existing authority. The "safety net" provided by such institutions – e.g., family and church – was destroyed from without, by state institutions taking on their roles, and from within, by the very members thereof refusing to acknowledge these structures and their roles within them. *For the classical liberal apotheosis of strict* (read: commutative) *justice leads to individualism and to the*

---

[70] *Problems of Poverty,* pp. 202–203.

[71] *Problems of Poverty,* p. 202.

emergence, in dialectical opposition, of an apotheosized distributive justice in the form of collectivist progressive liberalism.[72]

Confessional Religion and Justice

From the beginning it was not so. Western civilization had engendered a social order based equally on both the two principles of justice, commutative and distributive, strict and broad, or, if you will, group-external and group-internal. What is unique about Christianity – and this is the key – is likewise what it is that enabled this framework of justice and in fact the common-law system to develop as it did. From this root, and no other, did the social order as described in the previous chapter evolve.

Judicial Theology

For this understanding of justice is based in *judicial theology.* Such theology, anticipated by Augustine, was given explicit, albeit provisional, shape by Anselm, Archbishop of Canterbury from 1093 to 1109. In his dialogue *Cur Deus Homo,* "Why God Became Man," Anselm laid out the structure of justice in such a way as to explain the existence of mercy as well. In Christ, God became man, and He became man in order to satisfy, through His atoning work on the cross, both the claim of justice and the claim of mercy, by both paying for man's sins and by extending that payment to man so as to redeem him to restored relationship with God the Father.

The justice which was satisfied on the cross is strict justice, the

---

[72] We now know this as "social justice." But there is nothing social about social justice. It is merely distributive, and thus group-internal, justice extended illegitimately across society as a whole, thus entailing the displacement of commutative (group-external) justice and conversion of society into a monolithic organization. I hope DV to publish an extended critique of this concept in a forthcoming treatment.

justice of the *lex talionis*,[73] which no one can escape, it being grounded in the very nature of God. As jurists have long realized, the rigorous pursuit of this justice is impossible in the human condition, for it is insupportable: hence the warnings "Fiat justitia, pereat mundi" [Let there be justice, though the world perish] and "Summum jus, summum injuria" [Supreme right, supreme injury]. Through the atonement, however, this justice has been made amenable to human administration, its rigor being offset through the ministry of mercy: the ministry of the atoning work of the Messiah, extended first and foremost through the church, "Which is his body, the fulness of him that filleth all in all" (Ephesians 1:23).

Church and State as Coordinate Public Jurisdictions

Hence, in history the administration of strict justice was enabled and fomented precisely by the Western Roman church, who understood justice and law[74] because she understood justice and mercy. By means of her canon law, both as model and as counterpart, the church established a working framework of jurisdictions which, although not flawless by any means, put the state on its feet and enabled the growth of the common law as has been described in this book.[75] Within this framework of jurisdictions, the church reserved to herself the ministry of mercy, while calling upon the state to take upon itself the ministry of justice.

The distinctive and characteristic associationalism of Western

---

[73] "But if there is harm, then you shall pay life for life, eye for eye, tooth for tooth, hand for hand, foot for foot, burn for burn, wound for wound, stripe for stripe" (Exodus 21:23–25, ESV).

[74] The first title of Justinian's *Digest* was entitled "De Iustitia et Iure" (Of Justice and Law), and, in its train, many treatises of moral theology were likewise so entitled.

[75] Berman, *Law and Revolution,* is must reading in this regard.

civilization developed within the context of church and state exercising separate yet coordinate jurisdictions. Communes were formed which in turn became towns and cities; and various forms of association in the service of various individual goals – business, educational, vocational – flourished. This could happen precisely because of the existence of an integrating, universal order enabling the existence of a pluralism of associations, in which associationalism was allowed for by the method of sovereign confirmation of spontaneous organization and arrangement.[76] In turn, the distinctive *Ius Commune* developed as the jurists' expression of this universal order – although the reality constantly outpaced the theoretical accommodation thereof.

This explains the burgeoning interest in the Justinianian corpus right at the time in which the West was experiencing its renaissance of culture. Why was Roman law resorted to in order to develop this common law? Because, as Stahl has noted, Roman law realized the principles of strict justice by separating them out from morality and politics[77]; in this way it complemented the existing customary law, which itself was not simply jettisoned but supplemented in the areas in which it was lacking – precisely those institutions of external private law.[78]

---

[76] See the appendix, "The Common-Law Order."

[77] This is not to say that it did so infallibly. Elsewhere Stahl argued that while Roman law provided the indispensable factual parameters for positive law, i.e., the principle of the nature of the case, it did not define justice. This is because it did not recognize the difference between external private law and the internal law-orders of the associations being coordinated. This led to its one-sidedness, as Stahl describes. See *Private Law*, appendix: "The Value of Roman Law."

[78] Stahl, *Private Law,* appendix: "The Value of Roman Law"; furthermore,

Atonement and Liberty

So then, atonement made possible the administration of strict justice by the state, whereby the state restricts its activity primarily to the administration of this justice; and the church enabled it to do so, the church, who, recognizing the extent of the atonement, established her ministry of mercy in the midst of the social order, in so doing calling the state to its proper role as "the minister of God, a revenger to execute wrath upon him that doeth evil" (Romans 13:4).

The effect of the church on the state is forcefully expressed by the Dutch theologian A. A. van Ruler:

> *The state first attains its true essence through the church.* The state is de-demonized by revelation. Through the Word of God it turns from being a project and habitation of the gods into a servant of God.... It is quite a happening, one in which salvation truly takes place, when the state, through the mighty Word of God, is liberated from this delusion that it is the project and dwelling place of the gods, that it is God himself on earth, and from the barren paralysis of this delusion arises to real service as servant of God. To this end the state needs the church, the church as the bearer of the Word of God. And that does not happen just once, once and for all. That happens permanently. The church's action in the world is one continuous witch trial. Because the truth is unceasingly expressed, the world as God's creation and the state as God's servant is unceasingly kept going. In this manner life is guarded and saved. If the church disappears for a moment, then sooner or later the state must absolutize itself as God. And the last will be worse than the first. When the demons return to the house from which they

---

Dankwardt's important discussion, *Nationalökonomisch-civilistische Studiën* [Studies in Economics and Roman Law], pp. 28ff.

were expelled, the disaster is incalculable. These are things that, in my view, are easy to read from the history of Europe. Only put the names of Constantine the Great and Clovis at the beginning and the names of Lenin and Hitler at the end.[79]

"The only possible source of political liberty is on the premise of the atoning work of Jesus Christ."[80]

To the liberal, whether classical or progressive, this is anathema. Surely the state can be called upon to administer justice in this manner without any appeal to the supposed atoning work of Christ? But this is precisely what is wrong with secular theories of the state and of the role of religion in society. *Justice cannot be achieved until atonement is achieved.* Ancient societies perceived this, and made sacrifice – plant, animal, even human – an integral part of their public life. Modern man thinks he has escaped this necessity, relegating religion to the private sphere, secularizing the public square. This is pure self-deception.

Christ achieved just such atonement on the cross. This atonement is administered to the world through the ministry of mercy, exercised firstly through the ministry of Word and Sacrament, then the diaconate. Through this ministry the church makes her jurisdiction felt; and in so doing she makes room for the *proper* jurisdiction of the state, and for the various internal jurisdictions of a pluralistic social order. She reserves to herself the cure of souls and the exposition of ethics, restricting the role of the state to the civil sphere, thus civil private law and public law, while likewise referring to the rights and duties of men in the private spheres of life, mediating their jurisdictions vis-à-vis each other as well as an otherwise overweening state.

---

[79] *Religie en Politiek* [Religion and Politics], pp. 174, 175.

[80] Rushdoony, *Politics of Guilt and Pity*, p. 10.

Where the work of Christ's atonement is not acknowledged, justice falls to the ground. Justice floats on atonement and cannot exist apart from it. Justice receives its full depth and breadth in human life when it flows from mercy as expressed in the atonement, not when it is severed therefrom, for then justice can no longer be distinguished from mercy. At that point there commences the confusion of justice and mercy, of law and grace, of sin and crime, wherein the one consumes the other, obliterating the salutary distinction.

Modern apostasy began with the French Revolution – "Ni Dieu ni maître" – which, interestingly enough, chronologically accompanied the rise of the modern welfare state, as witness the revolution in the English poor laws.[81] Both were the fruit of the new philosophy of man whereby the individual becomes the source of law, and the institutions of civil society the source of evil. The result is the entitlement mentality, against which Thomas Chalmers tirelessly expostulated.[82] It is also the warped mentality which has given us political correctness and so-called cancel culture – the truly religious zeal to silence all conflicting opinions in the name of freedom of expression. Such zeal can only be seen against the background of the loss of religion in public life, for it is the zeal of the religious fanatic, aiming through the vehicle of the state and politics to achieve perfect justice and full atonement.[83]

The natural rights paradigm gave birth to the classical liberal. Far from the freedom of religion which this promised, it paved the way

---

[81] For a description of the earth-shaking transformation brought about here, see Polanyi, *The Great Transformation,* ch. 8, "Speenhamland." In addition, Chalmers' works are replete with the theme.

[82] See my *Common Law & Natural Rights,* ch. 7, "The Religious Root of the Social Question."

[83] For more on this theme, see *Common Law & Natural Rights,* ch. 8, "The Quest for Atonement"; R. J. Rushdoony, *Politics of Guilt and Pity.*

for the monstrosity of a totalitarian Moloch-worship such as confronts civilization today. This was accomplished by hamstringing Christianity, removing it and the church from the public square, either in the name of a vague civil religion or a will-o'-the-wisp neutrality. Study the history – there is perfidy underlying the incessant attacks on the church's role in public life, which by now has been repaid by the totalitarian movement which liberalism has since become. For "nature abhors a vacuum." The public square, evacuated of Christianity, cannot remain as such for long. It must have a religious grounding, if not in true religion, then in false.

Classical Liberalism's Delusions of Neutrality

The delusion entertained by classical liberals regarding the supposed blessing of state neutrality is clearly seen in Michael Novak's argument, made during the heyday of Reagan Republicanism, in favor of "the reverential emptiness at the heart of pluralism."[84] Novak thinks that Christians desire to "*command* the system" but need to recognize that they must "adjust to a role which removes them from command and places them outside the center" (p. 69).[85] As for

---

[84] *The Spirit of Democratic Capitalism,* p. 68.

[85] "Some Christian leaders can hardly help wishing to make theirs a Christian civilization.... Moreover, they are sorely tempted to do so directly, at the center, from the top, thoroughly. To think that they must attempt their important work only indirectly, by inspiring millions of individuals and through the competition of ideas and symbols in a pluralistic marketplace, must inevitably seem to some too demanding" (p. 69). This speaks to the utter misunderstanding of what a Christian social order is all about. Pluralist associationalism is precisely what Christianity fostered, as we have seen, to a degree not seen in any other society; the command-oriented polity is precisely what we get when we *abandon* Christianity. But Novak

Christian symbols, they "ought not to be placed in the center of a pluralist society. They must not be, out of reverence for the transcendent which others approach in other ways" (p. 70).

> In a genuinely pluralistic society, there is no one sacred canopy. By *intention* there is not. At its spiritual core, there is an empty shrine. That shrine is left empty in the knowledge that no one word, image, or symbol is worthy of what all seek there.[86] Its emptiness, therefore, represents the transcendence which is approached by free consciences from a virtually infinite number of directions. (Aquinas once wrote that humans are made in the image of God but that since God is infinite He may be mirrored only through a virtually infinite number of humans. No concept of Him is adequate.) Believer and unbeliever, selfless and selfish, frightened and bold, naive and jaded, all participate in an order whose *center* is not socially imposed (p. 53).

Nevertheless, he goes on to argue that the center of the US is not really empty – why, we have the Declaration of Independence to tell us that. "Human beings, according to the Declaration of Independence, are endowed with inalienable rights by the Creator. Abraham Lincoln and other presidents have freely reverenced the Almighty. On coins and notes of deposit one reads: 'In God we trust.'" Doesn't this mean that God is at the center? Well, yes and no.

> For those who so experience reality, yes. For atheists, no. Official religious expressions are not intended to embarrass or to compromise those who do not believe in God. They have a pluralistic content. No institution, group, or person in the United States is

---

and his ilk have run off with the purloined inheritance and cannot see where they got it from.

[86] *Sic!* From a supposed Christian!

entitled to define for others the content signified by words like "God," "the Almighty," and "Creator." These words are like pointers, which each person must define for himself. Their function is to protect the liberty of conscience of all, by using a symbol which transcends the power of the state and any other earthly power. Such symbols are not quite blank; one may not fill them in with any content at all. They point beyond worldly power. Doing so, they guard the human openness to transcendence (pp. 53–54).

This reminds us of President Eisenhower's telling description of American civil religion: "In other words, our form of government has no sense unless it is founded in a deeply felt religious faith, and I don't care what it is".[87] But "what it is" makes all the difference. For as we are witnessing daily, this approach to the transcendent "in other ways" is the recipe for Antichrist, for the state as God walking on earth. There is no neutral ground by which religion is relativized. *Religion is the relativizer.* When the center is evacuated of one religion, it does not stay that way. To repeat Van Ruler's words, "When the demons return to the house from which they were expelled, the disaster is incalculable." Which is why Novak's commandment to leave the center vacant is itself utterly vacuous.

Along the lines of Novak's argument, classical liberalism eliminated the strictures contained especially in the Reformed confessions of faith, which charge the civil magistrate to acknowledge and promote the true religion while removing and preventing false religion and idolatry. It did this in the name of freedom of religion.

---

[87] An informative and diverting exploration of the attribution of this statement is found in Patrick Henry, "'And I Don't Care What It Is': The Tradition-History of a Civil Religion Proof-Text," *Journal of the American Academy of Religion*, Vol. 49, No. 1 (March 1981), pp. 35–49. The quote is on p. 41.

What a deception! For the requirement to establish one religion and prevent another is not an option, to be taken up or laid aside at will; *it is a requirement.* The state *must* establish one religion or another, for that is the basis of its laws and of the *res publica,* the public affair.

So what has actually been the case? Take for example Article 36 of the Belgic Confession.[88] There it states that the civil magistrate is to "remove and prevent all idolatry and false worship; that the kingdom of antichrist may be thus destroyed and the kingdom of Christ promoted." This has been pilloried as a statement of Constantinianism[89] and intolerance, unbecoming a free society. But take a closer look, and this time turn it on its head – reverse the terms – and see if this is not what modern civil government actually does: "remove and prevent all *true* religion and right worship of God; that the kingdom of Christ may be thus destroyed and the kingdom of antichrist promoted." Is this not the modern condition with respect to the public square and, increasingly, the private sector as well? Article 36 is not a *command* so much as a *description*; implicit in its stricture is the understanding that the magistrate, if he does not promote the true religion, will inevitably promote a false one at the expense of the true one.

Nothing could describe more accurately the status of religion in modern public life than Article 36 of the Belgic Confession of Faith.

---

[88] For the parallel case of the Westminster Confession of Faith at the hands of American Presbyterianism, see North, *Political Polytheism,* pp. 546ff.

[89] See the appendix, "Constantinianism and Article 36."

CONCLUSION

There is no pre-existing condition of liberty in a supposed state of nature. There is rather a baseline condition of subjection, from which no human society is exempt. Liberty is achieved through a laborious process of, to use Burke's phrase, "progress in virtue," and it is gained within the context of sovereignty and private law, the two pillars of the common law. The institutions of civil society are the foundations of liberty; strip them away, and civilization reverts not to sovereign individualism but monolithic collectivism. Liberty is not natural, it is artificial. This does not mean that it is unnatural, for it is the product of centuries of growth. It is a garden plant, not a weed; it does not just grow, but must be nurtured.

The body of liberty which has undergone this growth process is a composition of liberties, the content of Burke's prescriptive constitution. It is not a body of pre-existing rights that governments are concocted to maintain, and that are restored in the overthrow of a corrupt government. In fact, those rights cannot have developed but through the instrumentality of sovereignty. They are therefore creatures of positive law. In this context, Stahl's strictures against natural law in favor of positive law are well taken.[90]

The locus of our contemporary "culture war" is the struggle for sovereignty. It has already begun in the attempt to establish the principle of universal jurisdiction as the basis for international relations. It is evident in the incessant attempts to establish global control over energy resources in the name of threats such as climate change and the need to eliminate the use of fossil fuels. It is evident in the struggle over immigration reform, not only in the US but in

---

[90] *Principles of Law,* Chap. 2, "Positive Law, Natural Law, Revealed Law."

Europe as well; for, as mentioned in the Introduction, the proponents of the legalization of illegal immigration justify their position on the basis of an alleged prior human right.

Sovereignty, law, and rights are indissolubly connected. The common law does not contradict sovereignty, it establishes sovereignty. And it establishes sovereignty at the level of the nation, the proper seat thereof by divine right. Real rights flow from this; they are derivative, not original. What is original is God's revealed law in Scripture.

It is time our eyes were opened to this. As it stands now, we all, wittingly or unwittingly, think in terms of the mechanism of apotheosized subjective right. The only difference between conservatives and progressives is the use to which they wish to put it. But at the end of the day, we are all liberals – we all believe in this project, which revolves around the sovereign individual. Which is why classical liberals continue to get beaten "like a drum" by progressive liberals: the inner logic of the mechanism favors progressivism.

Jefferson's formulation lifts the veil on this aspect of the mechanism: instead of the Lockean triad of life, liberty, and property, he put forward life, liberty, and the pursuit of happiness – this latter being an utterly unjurisprudential goal because amenable to a range of interpretations. Nevertheless, quite understandable and even necessitated in terms of the mechanism – how could it remain restricted to mere property? The final paragraph of the majority's opinion justifying its decision in Obergefell v. Hodges reads as a further elaboration of this pursuit of happiness, a paean to the Jeffersonian platitude, notwithstanding the dissenting opinion by Justice Antonin Scalia that it sounded more like "the mystical aphorisms of the fortune cookie."

Fortune cookies tell the future, and this jurisprudence is rife with predictive capacity. We are headed towards a world not only in which the family as traditionally construed is doomed, but also in which the church is doomed. For the teaching of the church with regard to homosexuality is now ipso facto discrimination, on the verge of being classified as hate speech. The same is in store for the Bible's teaching regarding marriage as the only legitimate context for sexuality, and for the binarity of male and female as its only legitimate form.

Dobbs v. Jackson stands athwart this development, but without offering a principled alternative, since it only attacks the fruit of the development but not the root: the mechanism of apotheosized subjective right.

But there is much more in store for our country and our world. Nationhood is being obliterated before our very eyes, and by the same mechanism. What else could possibly be the rationale behind the importation of entire populations of underclass citizens of foreign countries (e.g., 25% of the Mexican population)? It is more than just "cheap labor" (that panacea of our latest iteration of corporate capitalist exploiters), for with the wonders of modern trade deals, that labor can be accessed just as easily and at wages just as permanently reduced in their countries of origin. No, the demographic ticking time bomb that is set to go off as the baby-boom generation retires and transitions into a giant mass of non-working dependents was not enough; no, we need to import millions more of low-wage, unskilled workers better fitted to serve as a voting bloc for entitlements, forming yet another mass of insufficiently productive dependents. Just how many entitlements can our system bear? We will soon find out.

We have our rights mechanism to thank for this, because the rationale for these kinds of otherwise irrational policy choices lies precisely in the putative entitlement perceived to accrue to each individual person regardless of race, religion, sexual orientation, or whatever other criterion strikes the fancy. This entitlement is what government can guarantee, what gives it its raison d'être, until of course it runs out of the wherewithal to furnish the entitled with what they are entitled to according to the latest bulletin of instantly obvious, self-evident, ungainsayable, inalienable rights.

This is what has happened with one group which has been promised so much in terms of entitlement – the African American population. They have been promised everything, and how much is there to show for it? But no worry, any blame can be attached squarely to, well, Republicans, or the rich, or white people generally, or the police. Let it never be made known that their champions in the public square, the Democratic party, are the same ones who are allowing the importation of mass quantities of cheap labor competing precisely for the same jobs in the same labor market as many African Americans do, making it even more difficult for said African Americans to break out of the spiral of poverty and dependency. If they knew it was the Democratic party and its policy of open borders that helped to ensure an unemployment rate for black youths far in excess of other ethnicities, would they care? And if they knew that all the fomenting of racial discord and antagonism that has taken place in recent years has been done precisely to distract from this other policy so as to keep the voting coalition afloat – would they care? After all, the mechanism has us all in its thrall.

What we do know is that America as we know it is on life support. Nationhood itself is on life support. The end game for the people behind these developments is the drastic curtailment of national sovereignty, the conversion of sovereign nations into provinces administered by a global regime, holding out universal entitlement to the gullible masses, which can only be realized through universal jurisdiction.

This also entails the right to be free from pesky preaching about sin. Here, the mechanism directly confronts the church. Stalin once asked derisively, "The Pope! How many divisions has he got?" Our contemporary politicians and academics and members of the power elite ask themselves a similar question. "Christians! How many votes have they got? How many teachers in the public schools? How many professors? How many judges? How many CEOs? How many journalists? How many media moguls?" What is not said out loud is that the new regime comes with an alternative religion, an alternative schedule of sin and guilt, which likewise requires atonement, as in the form of drastic lifestyle curtailment to atone for the violations inflicted either on the victim-group *du jour* or on "the planet."

The trajectory should by now be clear. Unless and until the mechanism which is driving this version of the "end of history" is itself combated and defeated – in the halls of jurisprudence, the pillared shrines of justice, the chambers of deliberation, the groves of academia, through the revival of public Christian faith – we can already project where this too will end. Are we already too late? Regardless of that, we have this assurance: "But he that shall endure unto the end, the same shall be saved" (Matthew 24:13).

APPENDIX 1: CONSTANTINIANISM AND ARTICLE 36

And their office is, not only to have regard unto and watch for the welfare of the civil state, but also that they protect the sacred ministry, and thus may remove and prevent all idolatry and false worship; that the kingdom of antichrist may be thus destroyed, and the kingdom of Christ promoted. They must, therefore, countenance the preaching of the word of the gospel every where, that God may be honored and worshiped by every one, as he commands in his Word.

Article 36, clause 3 of the Belgic Confession of Faith

Our Netherland churches also are about to reconsider the article in our Confession which touches on this matter.

Abraham Kuyper, *Lectures on Calvinism,* p. 99.

The major objection that proponents of the "free church in the free state" make against Article 36 of the Belgic Confession is summarized in the term "Constantinianism." By this, two things are meant:

First, the inclusion of the entire church within a single church institute.

Constantine is held to have established the Christian religion as the religion of the state, and to have promoted the then-existing Christian church to the level of the state church – in other words, to have initiated what historians have come to call "Caesaropapism." It is the system in which citizenship and church membership are equivalent, in which the personnel of the church are state functionaries, in which the head of state is also head of the church.

While this may have been true for Byzantium, it was not for Western Christendom. The Roman Catholic church ruled out such a state church by its autonomous church government. Nevertheless, the evil lay precisely in unification within a single overarching institute. Abraham Kuyper put it like this:

> In Constantine's day, the attempt was made in an evil hour to seek the unity of the church of Christ in the unity of her organization. One government recognized by all the congregations on earth, one language spoken by all priests, one splendid liturgy would be the form of worship in all places of worship! Rome owes its rise and bloom to this lingering and devouring idea (*Vrijheid,* p. 15).

The Reformation broke with this overarching unifying institute, but – say the critics – it did not learn its lesson; instead, it reverted to a form of Caesaropapism. The unity of a single church institute was now established at the national level, resulting in the state church. Kuyper again:

> The work of the Reformation, however beautifully begun, ceased halfway. It was to bring freedom of the spirit, and it wreathed itself with laurels when only the freedom of the national church was guaranteed. This cannot be emphasized enough. Rome's unity embraced all lands and in every land every soul that confessed. When the curse of that unity made itself manifest, it was broken, but only halfway: yes, the former bond, not the latter. The people's church was made free from the universal church founded by Rome, but unity was maintained in that people's church. Thus Rome's evil, albeit on a smaller scale, returned to the national churches, and the idea of preserving the unity that had been found useless to the world, at least to maintain one's own heritage, proved so powerful that men of wise minds have not yet escaped her temptation

(*Vrijheid*, p. 16).

But the time of the state church has passed: "The state church has had her day. It may be asked whether she ever brought blessing. Now that every sphere of life is seeking its own form, her restoration is not even to be considered" (*Vrijheid,* pp. 8–9). And in the condition of pluriformity in which we now live, there is no way for the magistrate to decide which church institute is the true one. "And now we put to those who wish to maintain Article 36 unchanged – and they lack any right to participate further, as long as they have not answered it pertinently and conclusively – this question, dominating the whole dispute: How should the magistrate, if he finds more than one visible church on his terrain, decide which among the many is the *only true* one?" (*De Gemeene Gratie,* vol. III, p. 249).

Now then, such forced church unity in a single institute entails the *second* aspect of Constantinianism, the persecution of heretics. This second element was necessitated by the first. Kuyper again:

> This system of bringing differences in religious matters under the criminal jurisdiction of the government resulted directly from the conviction that the Church of Christ on earth could express itself only in *one* form and as *one* institution. This *one* Church alone, in the Middle Ages, was the Church of Christ, and everything, which differed from her, was looked upon as inimical to this one true Church. The government, therefore, was not called upon to judge, or to weigh or to decide for itself. There *was* only one Church of Christ on earth, and it was the task of the Magistrate to protect that Church from schisms, heresies and sects (*Lectures on Calvinism,* pp. 100–101).

Kuyper charged that the Reformation continued with this Constantinian and medieval policy, and this was enshrined in Article 36. As he put it in *Lectures on Calvinism* (p. 100):

The duty of the government to extirpate every form of false religion and idolatry was not a find of Calvinism, but dates from Constantine the Great, and was the reaction against the horrible persecutions which his pagan predecessors on the imperial throne had inflicted upon the sect of the Nazarene. Since that day this system had been defended by all Romish theologians and applied by all Christian princes.

And in *De Gemeene Gratie* [Common Grace] (vol. III, p. 95), he added:

This entire system was not a new discovery by the Reformed but the general sentiment of their time, against which only a few voices were raised in protest. It was the theory of Rome which was maintained for centuries, the error of which one did not yet discern. One drifted along with the current of the past and defended the received sentiment with the same arguments with which it has always been professed. One therefore cannot say that our fathers parroted the Roman opinion half-consciously. That was not the case. It was a received opinion which they themselves approved of, advocated, and broadly defended.

But were not the Netherlands a haven for those persecuted for their faith? Yes, but this came *despite* the church's adherence to Article 36:

The conflict with their deeper-lying principles only gradually came to light in practice, and to awareness in Reformed life. For notwithstanding that our fathers agreed unanimously with Article 36, including that difficult clause, the Netherlands became the cradle, not of persecution because of faith, but of freedom of conscience (*De Gemeene Gratie,* vol. III, p. 95).

Now then: These two positions – that Article 36 demands a single church institute such as is manifested in a state church, and that it mandates the persecution of heretics – constitute its supposed "Constantinianism."

There is nothing to either of these charges.

The Reformed church in the Netherlands, for which the Belgic Confession was one of the Three Forms of Unity (along with the Heidelberg Catechism and the Canons of Dort) never was a state church in the sense here intended. She never embraced the entire population and never attempted to do so. What she did do was occupy the public square as *the* church of the Netherlands, the church which spoke with one voice to the magistrate (and whether the magistrate listened was another matter). Other churches were tolerated, other faiths were allowed a private existence, but as far as the public square was concerned, the Dutch Reformed church as the representative of true religion was *recognized* (not established) by the magistrate.

It is of the utmost importance to recognize here that Article 36 discusses the question of *religion*, not of a church institute, which church should be selected, etc. Hoedemaker put it like this:

> According to our Confession, the civil government is to determine
> 1) which *religion* in the state is to be accepted into the commonwealth and as such is to be protected and administered with public authority;
> 2) which religion will be allowed and tolerated (*Article 36,* p. 121).

The Reformed church as the representative of the true religion became the *recognized* church of the polity. This then was not the same as an established church, and certainly not the same as a state church. Johan Huizinga characterized the Reformed church's position in the Dutch polity along these lines: "The reformed faith was never a state or established religion, as Anglicanism, for instance, is in England. It held sway in the State, was supported by the State and was even granted a kind of public monopoly; if you like it was the Church of the State, but it was never a state church in the full sense of the word" (*Dutch Civilisation in the 17th century*, p. 48).

Article 36, then, does not mandate the establishment of a single church institute. It is true religion, not the true church, of which it speaks. "The 'removal and prevention of heresy and false religion' of which the Confession speaks, therefore has nothing to do with Christian churches and sects separated from each other in this way or that, but with entirely different groups which, through their godless positions or what our fathers considered to be such, infringe on the honor of God. It *presupposes the freedom discussed above*, which is inseparable from the national Reformed church's viewpoint regarding faith and the work of the Holy Spirit" (Hoedemaker, *Article 36*, p. 122).

Kuyper's line of argument about the magistrate being at a loss to choose between multiple church institutes, therefore falls entirely to the ground.

What about the persecution of heretics? This likewise has to be understood in terms of the church's function as custodian of the spiritual dimension of the public square. Public power carries inherently within it the *requirement* to establish a certain religion and to order public affairs, and the law it enforces, in terms of that religion. For at bottom the *res publica,* the "public affair," is a shared ethical system, by which all who share a certain territory must abide. This is *sovereignty* in the strict sense, and it is inescapable. The law established by, and the institutions established for public power are expressions of that ethical system. And there is no ethical system without an ultimate ground upon which it stands. That ultimate ground, the source and the purpose and the goal of the ethical system, is religion.

This power is indeed inescapable, but it is also limited; it is restricted by the very fact that it is *public* power. According to Article 36, then, the "remove and prevent" function "not only can but must be restricted to *public life*, the sphere to be reckoned to the civil government" (*Article 36,* p. 122).

The flip side of this is freedom of conscience, which was recognized by the Reformed church and is in fact promoted by Article 36. "It is in conflict with history when the matter is so presented as if there were a pagan viewpoint which was first taken over by the Roman church, then by Protestantism, and which subsequently, gradually was supplanted by a more liberal sense and greater generosity. We already knew the reason behind not forcing faith or promoting it by fear and hope. This was the direct, obvious consequence that could be derived from the Confession itself" (*Article 36,* pp. 120–121).

As one example, the Leyden University professors' *Synopsis Purioris Theologiae* of 1625, which put it this way:

> Although the magistrate may prohibit his subjects from publicly slandering the religion that he approves, he may not obligate them to accept faith, i.e., the form of confession approved by public right, and to confess and render assurance of this before men. Faith arises through persuasion, not coercion. People should be left more to their own devices about religion than about anything else. The Christian magistrate must avoid nothing as much as the foolish, impetuous severity which nurtures hypocrites, and forces subjects to confess with their mouths without believing in their hearts (Disp. L. LIX.).

Kuyper does the Reformers a great disservice when he attributes to them a simple acquiescence in received opinion and practice regarding the treatment of heretics and freedom of conscience. How is it that the Netherlands became the cradle of freedom of conscience? The Arminians? Might it not be because of, not despite, the church's confession?

> What if that difficult clause in Article 36 showed that *it is precisely persecution on account of faith that is ruled out?* .... The opinion unjustly attributed [by Kuyper] to our fathers was in conflict not only with the underlying principles of the Reformed church, but with the entire Confession in its most obvious teachings. The civil government had to fulfill everything commissioned to it on its own terrain, public life. It was no lord of conscience, no taskmaster of faith.... Dr. Kuyper is mistaken when he attributes this opinion to the fathers, and therefore also when he attributes attachment to this opinion to the desire for imitation (*Article 36*, p. 41).

Article 36 certainly does require the civil magistrate to remove and prevent false religion and idolatry. But this is inescapable. It all depends on what is deemed to be false religion and idolatry. The modern liberal state exercises the function of Article 36 as faithfully as any Christian state ever did, only in inverse fashion. For it removes the *true* religion from the public square and prevents it from exercising any influence there – and it does so as a matter of high principle, precisely as Article 36 requires, only, as we said, in inverse fashion. Writing in 1901, Hoedemaker tellingly wrote that "The modern state does not tolerate the church on its [i.e., the public] terrain. It only knows of [private] clubs, societies, and foundations, and should one desire recognition before the law, it must come in these forms. Speaking of removal, it is not possible to suppress a moral person more effectively than our constitution does" (*Article 36*, p. 70). And with the advent of political correctness, cancel culture, and "wokeness" on the part of public institutions and public education, is it not thoroughly evident that Article 36, far from being a relic of the past, faithfully represents the scope of state power? In fact, it forms a salutary *restriction* on that power by its focus on the public sphere, protecting the private sphere from interference, contrary to the contemporary drive of activist ideologues to invade that sphere.

Hence, it is not a question of whether or not the civil magistrate will remove and prevent false religion and promote true religion. It is simply a question of *which* religion will be considered true, and thus promoted, and which will be considered false, and thus removed and prevented. This is the hard-fought lesson we have now learned.

APPENDIX 2: RIGHTS AND ECONOMICS

An Analysis and Critique of Eugen von Böhm-Bawerk's Treatise on the Economic Function of Rights

Eugen von Böhm-Bawerk (1851–1914) was perhaps the most influential theorist of capital in the Mengerian ("Austrian") school of economic analysis. His volumes on capital and interest gained a wide readership and great notoriety, instigating a plethora of responses both positive and negative. Those volumes were erected upon a foundation he laid back at the start of his intellectual career, in a short, ostensibly unpretentious[91] discussion of what he considered a necessary preparation for his future work on capital. The article was entitled "Rechte und Verhältnisse vom Standpunkte der Volkswirtschaftlichen Güterlehre" (English translation: "Whether Legal Rights and Relationships are Economic Goods"). It is an article that has been referenced a good deal, usually favorably, and just as quickly skipped over to get to the main course.

The reason for skipping over it is in a way quite obvious. As Schumpeter put it, the article "contains apparently only the detail

---

[91] At least, if the introduction is anything to go by: "However highly one may, on other points, esteem encomiums for originality, the author of these lines is anxious in this very matter to forgo praise on that score. Since it would seem to be true that, the more original a doctrine concerning such simple matters is, the more artificial it usually turns out to be, the author of these lines would prefer, by far, rather than appear as the originator of a new doctrine, to appear in the eyes of a large number of readers as a mere interpreter of well-known views...." Böhm-Bawerk (1962), p. 31.

of a very arid chapter," albeit dealing with "a few interesting methodological problems," marking "the first step in the direction of the problem to which Böhm-Bawerk's life work was to turn, the problem of the economic structure of capitalism."[92] The article is more than arid; it is tedious and at times positively numbing. But it provides the necessary background to understanding not only the derivation of Böhm-Bawerk's concept of capital, but also the crucial importance of rights to economic analysis.

What Böhm accomplished in "Rechte und Verhältnisse" is to lay bare the inextricable connection between goods broadly speaking (both material goods and services) and rights. He did so in order to come to a more precise definition of goods. He had realized that no progress could be made in the development of a theory of capital without first coming clean with this issue. The problem was that economists had developed a third category of goods besides material things and personal services, that of "rights and relations," a category which had gained greatly in importance with the development of the capitalist economy, and which included such things as stocks, bonds, copyright, goodwill, patents, and the like. Were such phenomena, "the mass" of which, as Henry Macleod assures us, "exceeds many times the mass of Corporeal Property,"[93] really to be considered economic goods in their own right, alongside tangible goods and services?

Böhm's conclusion is unassailable: such rights cannot be considered economic goods. But did he, after coming to this conclusion, build upon it by drawing proper inferences? I shall argue that he did not; and that it is in fact the inferences that he drew, so plausible at first sight, which led to insoluble difficulties not only in his own theory of capital but that also have helped to foster the illusion that

---

[92] Schumpeter (1952), p. 571.
[93] Macleod (1881), vol I, p. 168.

capital theory is about a "homogeneous and quantifiable capital stock" or "homogeneous aggregate."[94] His conclusions have helped to realize a divorce between capital theory and actual practice, the business practice of capital accounting. Ludwig von Mises took an entirely different view, and it enabled him to develop his argument of the necessity of capital accounting to the functioning of the economy.

This article will begin with a detailed summary of Böhm's "Rechte und Verhältnisse" – to the author's knowledge, the first such summary ever published – before subjecting it to a thorough analysis and evaluation. Implications of this evaluation for capital theory, and specifically for comprehending the achievement of Ludwig von Mises, follow thereafter.

Rechte und Verhältnisse – Summary and Analysis

Böhm's purpose in this article is to clarify the concept of economic goods. A necessity, he felt, for the concept of economic goods had become hopelessly confused, and it is economic goods that form the subject matter of economic theory. Böhm set out to answer this question as a preliminary exercise to clear the way for his own theory of capital and interest. For capital theory, he argued, concerns itself with economic goods of a specific kind, to wit, material goods.[95] Therefore, in order to develop a theory of capital he had first to come to an understanding regarding economic goods.

Böhm starts out by referencing an error that everyone[96] agreed was an error – the case of Henry Macleod's "double counting" of economic goods. Macleod, he argued, had made the mistake of

---

[94] Lachmann (1956), pp. 6, 53.

[95] Böhm-Bawerk (1930), p. 10.

[96] "It encountered virtually universal and unanimous rejection." Böhm-Bawerk (1962), p. 35.

counting e.g. a loaned good and the right to repayment of the same loaned good as two different economic goods. "The premises on which MacLeod's syllogism is based can be expressed in two short sentences, viz: (a) when A lends B a dollar, then B possesses in that dollar a corporeal thing having the value of a dollar; (b) in his claim to the repayment of the dollar A possesses an intangible or nonmaterial good possessing a present value approximating one dollar which is not identical with the corporeal dollar itself."[97] The untenability of such a doctrine is self-evident, he argues. But, and this is Böhm's point here, Macleod was only following through to its logical conclusion a certain widely-held conviction on the part of economists: that rights could be economic goods alongside corporeal goods and personal services.

Wilhelm Roscher, the dean of 19th century German economists, is his prime example. On the one hand Roscher argues against Macleod's method; but on the other he counts "relationships to persons and things," loans, etc., as intangible goods. Then, in order to avoid double-counting, Roscher argues that these rights are only to be counted as goods from an individual's standpoint, and not from the standpoint of the broader economy. Not good enough, says Böhm. Either rights are economic goods to all or they aren't at all; and he then sets himself the task of elucidating what in fact economic goods actually are.

A good is a thing that serves human needs. "Goods, in the economic sense of the word, are those things which *serve human beings as the means or tools for the attainment of their personal well-being.*"[98] Elaborating on the scheme put forth by Menger before him, Böhm argues that an economic good must meet five criteria: 1) there must be a human need it can serve; 2) it must be objectively suitable to

---

[97] Böhm-Bawerk (1962), p. 35.

[98] Böhm-Bawerk (1962), p. 39.

bring about the mediate or immediate satisfaction of that need; 3) people must recognize this suitability to satisfy the need; 4) people must be capable of putting this suitability to satisfy a need to use; and 5) finally, there must be the power to utilize the good such that it can in fact be applied to the satisfaction of the need.[99] What is clear from this is that goods-quality is not inherent in a thing but rather depends largely on the activity of the subject, of the goods-utilizer; goods-quality is subjective. A good can only be a good to a determinate subject; there is no such thing as absolute goods-quality. The person in question must have a need; he must recognize that the thing in question is capable of satisfying that need; he must be able to apply the good to that need; otherwise it is a thing merely, and not yet a good. "Strictly speaking, then, one should never speak simply of goods as such, but always only of *goods for X or for Y or Z, or other specific economic subjects.*"[100]

Many "things" taken to be goods, i.e., of use to people, are not goods in the economic sense. Böhm summarizes the lists he has come across, which included "*personal services, love, the organized state, the church, virtue, character* (as a means to the establishment of credit – Macleod), *honor, investors' patents, the Iliad* (Rossi), *the security bestowed by the law, monopolies, the joy of demolition* (*De Augustinis*; quoted by Roscher in *Grundlagen*, p. 106), *counsel and advice, good health, strength, cleverness, 'good sense,' knowledge, good taste, companionability, freedom, ownership, morality, the relationship of a commanding officer to his soldiers* (Roscher), *credit* (Macleod), *claims* (Hufeland and Roscher), *the 'utilization of a good'* (Hermann)."[101] Those things which although useful do not correspond with the criteria established earlier cannot be considered

---

[99] Böhm-Bawerk (1962), pp. 42–43.

[100] Böhm-Bawerk (1962), p. 43.

[101] Böhm-Bawerk (1962), p. 50.

economic goods. "The only things that can have validity as economic commodities are the useful services which become available
through those persons and those qualities and powers. It is these
alone which can function as independent entities in economic life
and become the object of consumption, of exchange, of rental, and
thus in all essential respects play the rôle of goods."[102]

Now then, what of this third category of goods alongside material things and personal services? After all, they play a direct and
indisputable role in economic life. "Claims are conveyed, rental
rights are bought at a price, namely, the rent that is paid. Goodwill
often attains very real money value, no matter whether it depends
on purely factual circumstances (such as the high repute of a firm's
name) or on specific legal rights (such as patent rights or a granted
monopoly). Phenomena such as these would seem to offer most per-
suasive evidence of the genuine goods-quality of nonmaterial
things."[103] Much opposition has been raised to this inclusion of immaterial things in the list of economic goods. But that should not
be surprising. Even though we may heartily disown a materialistic
view of the universe and recognize the significant role of the ideal
in our lives, still we must accept that a true good must have a power
to satisfy needs in and of itself. Does a relationship have such a character? "When we consider such a thing as *2:3* or *x:y* – and all relationships really possess the same nature as these ratios or should we,
rather, say, the same lack of nature? – when, I say, we consider such
things, and are asked to accept them, not merely as representative of
goods, but as actually *being* goods, that demand will doubtless always remain one of those things which, for lack of something better
we accept as an expedient, 'for the sake of argument,' but toward

---

[102] Böhm-Bawerk (1962), p. 51.
[103] Böhm-Bawerk (1962), p. 52.

which, to the very end, we retain ineradicable reservations."[104]

This explains the visceral opposition to considering immaterial things to be goods.

The Nature of Rights

In order better to understand this situation, Böhm moves on to examine the nature of legal rights. He sets out to describe the role of rights, in particular property rights, with respect to economic goods. What is crucial to the utility of economic goods is that they be in the possession of the beneficiary of the good, either currently or in prospect, otherwise they are of no use to him. Physical possession is thus the primary thing; but this must be maintained by one's own hand, and thus is an uncertain affair. In an environment where the rule of law prevails, the power of the state backs up possession, making it more secure, while also guaranteeing the prospect of possession by enforcing contracts. Thus, rights are simply guarantees by the legal order of the main thing, possession. Both legal and physical control are necessary to making things goods. "Not until they are combined do legal and physical control constitute that fully assured power of disposal which is demanded by our economic interests and which, as we have already seen, bestows on the useful things in question their goods-character and makes them for us genuine goods."[105] "Legal title to a thing, like the physical possession of it, does not develop outside of, and in addition to the good to which it applies, so as to become a second, independent good. It simply helps to make the thing a good in the first place."[106]

---

[104] Böhm-Bawerk (1962), p. 53.

[105] Böhm-Bawerk (1962), p. 59.

[106] Böhm-Bawerk (1962), p. 62.

So much is clear; but then the theorists took a wrong turn.[107]

> ... In fact it is so clear that it could not have been denied, if one had just singled out property-rights-to-things from the sphere of the remaining asset rights [Vermögensrechte] and, using this example, had investigated and settled the question as to whether "rights" could be independent goods. That however has not been the case. Those investigations rather as a rule used as paradigm a right that did not cover its object so visibly and completely as does the right of property, but instead appeared to maintain an independent existence and validity [Geltung] as is the case with e.g. rights of obligation [contract, tort] or servitudes; and these became the temptation to prepare in principle an independent place for "rights" in the world of goods.

Property rights should have been used as the paradigm case, for what is true of property is true, economically speaking, of other rights as well. Property provides a complete degree of control over the good in question, while other rights provide a greater or lesser degree of control in accordance with their specific character; the difference between property rights and other rights is not in kind but in degree, quantitative not qualitative. Of course, the law has to treat these rights as different in kind in accordance with specifics as to how they are to be enforced; but economically speaking they are all on the same line. And if property rights are not to be counted as goods alongside the object of the right, then neither is any other right.

Böhm now turns to investigate more precisely what it is about goods that makes them goods, and what role rights play in this

---

[107] The following quotation I translate in full, because the Huncke translation of this particular passage is misleading. The parallel passage in the Hunke translation is on pp. 62–63.

process. He observes that what is economically important with regard to material goods is not the goods per se but the useful services [Nutzungen] that they provide. Every good provides such services, and it is these services that economically are the important thing, not the things in themselves. These renditions of services are the primary objects of rights. And it is for these renditions of service that goods are valued; they do not possess value in themselves. "It is not goods, but it is in very truth the renditions of service which emanate from those goods which constitute the smallest independent units of our economy and that the former (i.e., goods) constitute only complexes of the latter, that goods are therefore a secondary category."[108]

Jurisprudence recognizes these renditions of service. When title to the entire bundle of these renditions of service is provided, one has a right of property; when title to only a greater or lesser amount of the total is provided, one has a servitude or other real right, or a personal right, a right to personal service. Separate restricted bundles make up the objects of these restricted rights. Such rights are not to be considered economic goods – it is their objects that are goods. "The distinguishing feature of all these rights is as follows. The person possessing the right has control, not of the total number of renditions of service of which the object of his legal relationship is capable, but is limited by some line of demarcation setting apart some portions of the renditions which alone are subject to the control and disposal of the possessor of the right."[109]

The upshot of this discussion is that there is no need to make room for a third category of goods, rights and relations, to take into account these restricted bundles of renditions of service. These bundles are derivations of the two main categories of goods, material

---

[108] Böhm-Bawerk (1962), p. 77.
[109] Böhm-Bawerk (1962), p. 80.

goods and personal services. They do not form a third category, and neither do the rights for which they form the object.

This takes care of that category of rights Böhm refers to as "rights to partial utilization." He then moves to discuss rights to the future yield of goods. The first kind of such right is the right of repayment of a loan. Such a right does not provide secure possession of a good, in the way property rights do; it provides no possession at all, only the promise of possession at some time in the future. This leads to an odd divergence: the owner of the lent good no longer has the good in his possession – "at the moment he possesses *no good at all*;"[110] it is the borrower who possesses it. Yet for all that his claim to future repayment is itself an object of wealth, it can be traded, it has market value. And on the other hand, the actual possessor of the good does not, in it, possess any wealth.

The Problem of Accounting

Posing the problem like this leads Böhm into a new area of discussion, and one of momentous importance to the future development of capital theory: that of the computation of wealth. This is the subject matter of accounting.

Accounting, Böhm argues, is a very inexact art. It attempts to pin down the future value of goods. As such it is a hit-or-miss proposition, a matter of probabilities, since no one can estimate what the value of present goods will be at a certain point in the future. And yet, accounting attempts to do exactly this: to attribute value to e.g. goods the possession of which is not yet certain but only promised in the future. People think that because something which isn't even in existence yet (e.g., contracted work) is attributed present value, it must be a good; but what accountants do is not necessarily "economic" – their entries in the books are not necessarily goods per se.

---

[110] Böhm-Bawerk (1962), p. 85.

What has happened with the explosion of new forms of wealth like shares, servitudes, patents, copyrights, goodwill etc. is not that goods have been expanded beyond material objects and personal services, as these still cover all possible goods, but that there has been an explosion in ways to account for these goods as assets.

There are therefore two categories which must be kept strictly separate: materials of wealth and forms of wealth. Materials of wealth are the actual goods and services; forms of wealth are subjective appraisals of those materials in accordance with varying circumstances, motives, considerations. The materials of wealth remain the same; the forms of wealth vary in accordance with the perspective of the observer. And this perspective is subject to distortion. "[There come] into existence *forms of wealth* as the multifarious aspects under which one and the same *material of wealth* presents itself subjectively to our imagination--an imagination, I would add, which is prone to indulge in subjecting the factual situation to subjective coloration, to biased interpretation, and even to downright distortion."[111]

It is the materials of wealth which are the essence; the forms vary. "Goods-quality only attaches to the core which underlies them."[112] And the multiplication of forms of wealth in modern life does not mean that the materials of wealth have multiplied. It is only the ways in which they are represented that have multiplied. "I consider them peculiar *computation-forms* which under certain presuppositions we are accustomed to apply to goods of the common kinds."[113]

So we have goods on the one hand, and computation forms on the other. A balance sheet, Böhm avers, lists both indiscriminately. But this should not confuse as to the actual state of affairs. The

---

[111] Böhm-Bawerk (1962), p. 97.

[112] Böhm-Bawerk (1962), p. 97 (grammar improved by the author).

[113] Böhm-Bawerk (1962), p. 98.

computation forms are only another way of taking into account that original category of goods, they do not set up a separate category of goods in addition to those already established, to wit, material goods and personal services.

Böhm then turns to apply these propositions to specific cases. In the case of asset calculation of goods we possess, such as books, coats, etc., it is a simple affair: they are simply listed as such. Then there are goods the value of which we expect at some point in the future: "such as winter clothing or ice skates in the summer, travel equipment, the prospective bride's 'hope chest,' future reserves of all sorts of goods."[114] Böhm claims that this is a simple affair; we simply list the material good as an object of wealth and assign to it the value of its future utility. Similarly with a good that has both present value and future value, such as a house, furniture, paintings, musical instruments. There future utility is assured, and the value of it is added to the value of the present utility; the good is assigned the capitalized value of its utilities both present and future.

Capital is a third case and a more difficult one. Capital consists in goods of so-called remoter orders, goods used in the production of other goods, standing at one or more removes from the finished product. There are two rules to keep in mind in regarding such goods: firstly, that their quality as goods depends on whether the end-product they help to produce is itself an economic good; and secondly that their value is determined by the value of the end-product.[115]

The value of capital goods is therefore derivative. The present value of capital goods depends on the value of the eventual product, but this is uncertain. The computation of this value is a thorny question (in fact, it is perhaps the crucial question in the development

---

[114] Böhm-Bawerk (1962), p. 99.
[115] Böhm-Bawerk (1962), p. 102.

of capital theory):

> The value of goods of remote order is, accordingly, a derived value. But at the same time it is a value that is prospective in nature and that anticipates the facts. This brings us back to our narrower problem of the computation of wealth. It is anticipatory for the following reason. Since the attainment of ultimate utility by way of consumption, which is what we look for in goods of remoter order, demands a transmutation of those goods of remoter order into goods of less remote order, and since it therefore calls for processes which can take place only in the course of time, those goods of remote order represent, in our computation of wealth, a future utility; and the value that is placed upon them (a value which is only a derived value, accruing to them only through the mediation of goods of less remote order and hence a value that is derived from the final common utility) is nothing but the form (the third form according to my enumeration) in which an indirect future advantage enters into the computation.[116]

Thus capital goods are valued in terms of future utility. Even though they are goods, they derive their value from the anticipated future value of the product, to the production of which they contribute. So this future value is anticipated and ascribed to these capital goods. This is, Böhm says, a third "form" of valuing goods in present possession but the value of which will be realized wholly or in part in future, the "form... in which an indirect future advantage enters into the computation."

Böhm now moves from describing these three categories of material goods to three other categories, not of material goods but of personal services ["forms of linkage" – German *Verknüpfungsformen*], not amenable to the above-mentioned "simple" forms of

---

[116] Böhm-Bawerk (1962), p. 104.

computation, because of the lack of a "real mediator of future advantage," i.e., possession of the material good which is to provide the future advantage. In these cases, one cannot list any present possession, because the future advantage is expected from a specific person or persons, and slavery no longer being in practice, the persons themselves cannot be considered possessed objects. Böhm lists three cases here (cases 4–6, following cases 1–3 above): 4) a person is obligated in a sufficiently secured manner to perform a future labor or other personal useful service; 5) future renditions of service from a certain object, otherwise owned by someone else, are attributed to an interested party other than the owner by virtue of a right specifically directed toward that end; 6) the future delivery of a material good or material renditions of service is expected through the agency of a person's service.

Rights and Economic Goods

Case 6 in particular is of great importance, for it includes all claims [Forderungen] and credit relations. Now then, since the obligated person cannot himself be listed as an asset, how are we to account these cases? What form of computation will we use? The expedient that has been hit upon is to name the right, the title to that future personal service, as a present good. But it is here that our problem has arisen. For in speaking of rights to future performances as if they were present goods, we have fostered the notion that these rights are things in themselves, with an autonomous value all their own. And it is jurisprudential practice which has fostered this device. "By sharply differentiating rights from the material things to which they applied, by designating them as '*incorporeal things*,' by speaking of the origin, the transfer, the encumbrance, the destruction of rights in a 'tone of voice' as if a right were an entity, a sort of being, the law brought it about that gradually in their conception of the conduct of practical affairs men became oblivious of the fact that rights do not belong in the category of *things* at all, but in that of *relationships*." And so have rights come to play the role of things, to be considered a good or an object of wealth. "One who speaks thus is never speaking the literal truth. A right can be only a variant of a *computation form*; it can never be the name of an independent *material of wealth*."[117]

These rights are therefore computation forms to take into account the assured future performances which they reference; they are another category of computation form in addition to those forms analyzed earlier, of goods presently owned by the value of which will be realized at some point in the future.

To Böhm, all of this should be self-evident, to the point that he feels he must apologize for wearying his reader. But it is necessary to go through the process, he says, because he still feels he will have to face the united opposition of jurisprudence and economics for drawing such-like conclusions, especially the jurists, "who so very long ago proceeded along this line of thought only to arrive at a point where *rights* and *things* came to be looked upon as coordinate entities and where the former were elevated to the rank of *res incorporales*,"[118] a distinction which, when understood as goods (*res corporales*) vs. rights (*res incorporales*) is nonexistent. "There was a failure to observe that where *rights* were observed to exist, there, of necessity, *goods* had to exist, too – goods which, by virtue of the rights, were also bound up with wealth; and there was a similar failure to observe that where only *things* were observed to exist and were designated as objects of wealth, there were also *rights* as well – rights applying to those very things – rights of the most complete and effective kind which, in turn, were bound up with those same things

---

[117] Böhm-Bawerk (1962), 112.

[118] Böhm-Bawerk (1962), pp. 114–115.

– that is to say, were bound up with wealth.[119]

And Böhm gets to the heart of the matter, expounding the true nature of the relationship between rights and goods, and the conclusion that must be drawn: rights such as patents and copyrights must never be considered goods in their own right, no matter how tenuous the connection with the good or service in question may be – for they always are attached to some good or other, and the key is always to keep that in mind.

The true nature of a right is that it is, as it were, the shadow of a good – "the juridical shadows which real corporeal goods cast upon the image of our wealth." The closer the relationship of the good to the right, the easier it is to recognize the shadow for what it is. And vice versa: the farther the right from the object of the right – the good – the more difficult it is to discern the connection. "That is how it happens that, the more complicated certain legal relationships are, and the more indefinite, the more difficult to perceive and the more subject to indirection in their acquisition are the true goods which a 'right' promises to deliver to us, the more general and the more pronounced is the disposition on the part of the economic theorists to declare the rights to be independent goods and, finally, that is how it is that just where those conditions are present in the highest degree (the field of patent rights and copyrights) the recognition of the independent goods-character of rights is accepted without exception."[120]

Lastly, Böhm turns to consider those "relations" which economists had become habituated of listing as economic goods.[121]

---

[119] Böhm-Bawerk (1962), p. 115.

[120] Böhm-Bawerk (1962), pp. 115–116.

[121] The connection between such relations and the actual goods and services to which they refer is even more tenuous than in cases 4–6 above. He

He concludes by reiterating what he considers to be the obvious result of this investigation: that rights can never be placed on a line with goods, because rights always have goods as their object, and goods always function as the substrate for rights. Therefore rights can never be considered goods in themselves.

This conclusion will not have any effect on economic practice, Böhm avers, because people will continue to count rights to repayment and the like as assets, and therefore they will continue to play the role of substitute for the underlying reality, which is goods and services and only goods and services. But economic *theory* cannot allow itself this kind of sloppiness. Now the use of metaphors is unavoidable in speech, and therefore it will be impossible to banish this manner of speaking even in discussions of theory. But Böhm feels he must in this context make a request: "that economic theory, *when it speaks* ex cathedra *about goods and categories of goods, substitute the two underlying associates, material goods and renditions of service, for the figurative appellations,* 'intangible rights' *and* 'relationship-goods.' *And I make the further request that, whenever it does employ figures of speech in mentioning these things as goods, it remain at least tacitly conscious of the figurative nature of its expressions.*"[122]

Evaluation

The conclusion is clear: rights cannot be equated with goods.

---

lists three examples: goodwill, which is the promise on the part of a potential competitor not to compete for customers; the state, which some had listed as a relation and as such an economic good; and love and friendship, which likewise had been listed as an economic good. As there is nothing in Böhm's discussion here which adds to what he has already said in regard to goods-nature and the role of rights therein, it should be safe to skip from here to the conclusion.

[122] Böhm-Bawerk (1962), p. 135.

Modern critics of Böhm's approach have disputed this conclusion. They see in it the portent of Böhm's materialistic capital theory and a deviation from Carl Menger's subjective approach to economic analysis.[123] They therefore argue in favor of restoring the *status quo ante*, of retaining the conception of goods put forward by the likes of Roscher, with rights put on a line with material goods and services, as a third category of goods. But, if one chooses this path, one must deal with Böhm's initial criticism. In other words, does one not then become guilty of the double-counting which got Böhm started in the first place? It would seem so. One must get beyond Böhm's critique if one wishes to critique him. Ignoring his challenge is a step backward.

The present author agrees with Böhm, that goods and rights are different kettles of fish. Nevertheless, there is a problem with Böhm's entire analysis, and it has to do with his very premise, the premise upon which he built the entire structure both of his analysis here and his great thesis regarding capital and interest. And that is this: that the true subject matter of economics is goods. That is not the case. Economics does not have to do, at least directly, with goods per se, but with assets. And these are not the same thing. Böhm thinks so, and he is not the only one. This is the underlying presupposition of all the discussions to which he refers, and the root of the error to which they all tend.

What then are assets if they are not goods? It is important in this context to keep in mind the German word for assets: *Vermögen*. Not only is this word important to economics, it is to jurisprudence as well. And it is the vital background to Böhm's own discussion, which after all took place in the Austro-German context.

In the German jurisprudential tradition, *Vermögen* is the central concept in private law, for in that tradition all rights of property

---

[123] Endres (1997), Gloria-Palermo (1999).

together with rights of contract and even tort are brought under one heading, originally the law of "things" – *res* – or assets (*Vermögensrecht*).

This is the path laid out by Roman law. Gaius devoted Book II of his *Institutes* to "*de rebus*," and Justinian's *Institutes* follow suit, Book II being entitled "*de rerum divisionis*," on the classification of things. Now the things that are of importance in private law are the things belonging to the *patrimonium*.[124] Patrimonium is one of the Roman equivalents for wealth, assets, *Vermögen*.

What are the things belonging to a *patrimonium*? Here we have the origin of Böhm's *bête noire*, the *res incorporales*. Justinian (1932) put it thusly (Book II, Title 2):

Again, some property [*res*] is corporeal, and some incorporeal.

(1) Corporeal property is such as by its nature is tangible; as, for instance, land, a slave, clothing, gold, silver, and in short, innumerable other things.

(2) Incorporeal property is that which cannot be touched, and is such as consists of rights; for instance, an inheritance, an usufruct, or obligations contracted in any way. Neither is it necessary that corporeal property should be included in an estate, for the crops gathered from land are corporeal, and what is due to us by reason of any obligation is ordinarily corporeal, for example, land, a slave, or money; while the right of inheritance itself, the right to make use of the crops, as well as the right of the obligation are incorporeal.

(3) To the same class belong rights attaching to urban and rustic estates, which are also called servitudes.

---

[124] Things outside of someone's *patrimonium* are either held in common or are owned by no one, such as the ocean. Another category, of sacred and religious goods, are a category unto themselves.

Apparently Böhm is justified in his criticism, for here we by all appearances have material and immaterial, corporeal and incorporeal "things" [*res*] put on a line.

But what are these "things" actually? Are they economic goods in the sense Böhm means?

They are not, and there's the rub. "Thing" in Roman law, as the above quotation implies, does not refer directly to goods, but rather to the rights attached to those goods.

Recall the description Böhm gives to rights with respect to goods: they are the shadow of goods, they represent goods, while goods in turn are the substrate of rights. All of this we can accept as true. Now the "thing" in Roman law is not the legal object – the good to which the right refers – rather, it is the right. That much is apparent from the above quotation from the *Institutes*. The translation of *res corporales* as "corporeal property" is an accurate one, for *res* in this instance refers to the *right* of property, *not* to the *object* of that right of property.

Böhm is not the only one confused by the Roman doctrine of *res*. The Roman jurists themselves were not always clear about what they meant with it. They did not always refer consistently to the property right; often they spoke directly of the object of the property right, which is this or that economic good. And they did so for precisely the reason Böhm indicated when he argued that property rights should have been used for the paradigm case in speaking of rights vis-à-vis goods: that the right of property completely covers, completely coincides with, the object to which it refers. Therefore one easily and insensibly slips from speaking of a property right to speaking of the object of the property right without being aware of having made that transition. But that does not take away from the fact that in the end they meant rights, not goods, when they referred to *res corporales* and *incorporales*.

The eminent German legal philosopher Rudolph Jhering made

some pertinent comments which are illuminating in this regard:

> Exchange when viewed from the perspective of jurisprudence is not the circulation of things [*Sachen*] but a transfer of rights. The thing apart from the right is worthless; a good's worth is not determined simply by its economic usefulness or applicability but essentially by its applicability being legally secured, and by the manner in which it is so secured. Law is an essential factor in the concept of value, which is why all values suffer during a revolution and rise again with the return of legal security. The transfer of a thing is the juridical transfer of a right; traffic in goods is the juridical founding, transfer, cessation of rights.[125]

Jhering applies this reasoning to the case at hand, showing that such a conclusion is clouded when only property rights are considered, because the right and the thing so completely coincide. And this is what misled the Roman jurists.

> The justness of this observation becomes immediately apparent everywhere where a right to a thing other than property, in which the right and the thing cover each other, is ordered or transferred. With property, outwardly it is the thing which is transferred, and a conception which cleaves to outward appearance can easily overlook the inward occurrence – the transfer of the right – or confuse it with the outward appearance. This is what happened in the older Roman law. To it, property transfer was not the transfer of property but of the thing. The transfer of the right itself as a thing of objective ideal existence to be detached from the previous holder was too pointed, too abstract for it; it conceived of the course of events involved in the transfer of property as the previous owner

---

[125] Jhering (1874), vol. II, p. 437. My translation.

yielding the *thing*, the new owner taking hold of it.[126]

The true state of affairs is this: assets or wealth, *patrimonium*, *Vermögen*, are not composed of goods, as Böhm assumed; they are composed of rights, which always and everywhere have Böhm's goods as their objects. But, and this is the point: goods in and of themselves are never listed as asset *components*, they are always considered asset *objects*, the objects to which the assets refer. *Assets are rights*.

German jurists therefore developed the distinction between *Vermögensbestandteilen*, asset components, and *Vermögensobjekten*, asset objects. It is the former to which the Roman *res*, both *corporales* and *incorporales*, belong. The latter are the economic goods to which they refer. And this explains why one of the main headings of German private law was the law of assets (*Vermögensrecht*), characterized by Stahl as the law of property in the broad sense,[127] comprising the law of property, of contract, and of tort.

This state of affairs was concisely laid out by a contemporary of Böhm's, Paul Oertmann, in his important work on *The Economic Doctrine of the Corpus Juris Civilis*.[128] Referring not only to Böhm's article but also to the work of Romanist jurists like Windscheid and Dernburg, Oertmann explodes the entire methodology introduced by the economists of putting goods and rights on a line.

> [With the distinction between *res corporales* and *incorporales*] the Romans did not intend to classify asset *objects* but only asset *components*. To include servitudes, obligations and the like among the latter is entirely correct. But in order to be consistent, the most important, comprehensive asset right, property, should also be

---

[126] Jhering (1874), II, pp. 437–438.

[127] Stahl, *Private Law*, pp. 43ff.

[128] Oertmann (1891).

included here, because it is not the *thing* itself which is a *component* of our assets – this is much rather its object – but only the *legal relation* to the thing: that is what property is. And this is the weak point of the entire distinction. Enticed by the general habit of thinking and speaking in daily life which falsely substitutes the possession of an object for possession of a right to that object, the Roman jurists identified the right of property with the thing, a confounding which is understandable in the strict development of the Roman law of property but which makes it no less theoretically objectionable. The *proper* contradistinction could only be property – servitudes – obligations (asset components) on the one hand and things – persons c.q. performances (asset objects) on the other; the mixture of the two categories can only lead to a hopeless logical blunder.[129]

Oertmann lays out the proper method of categorization here. One must deal either with rights or with goods, but one cannot and must not confuse the two. When dealing with rights, the proper arrangement is property rights, other real rights, and obligations (contract, tort). When dealing with goods, the arrangement is material things and personal services. The former are asset components, the latter asset objects. Only asset components belong to assets proper; to list asset objects as assets is to confuse the categories.

Which is precisely what the economists, and certain jurists following them, had done.

The reigning economic doctrine defends the contrary, either in Roscher, who directly connects his teaching with the traditional Roman *divisio*, or, as with Wagner, who independently develops an entirely analogous division of goods. Roscher counts as goods: (1) persons or personal services;

---

[129] Oertmann (1891), pp. 29–31. My translation.

(2) things;

(3) relations to persons or things – res incorporales, such as clientele, name, and the like; things, of course, which have meaning only for private assets, not for general wealth [Weltvermögen].

Now this division deals only with what we earlier concluded to be *goods*, that is, asset objects. Not only economists but jurists as well so conceive the Roman division.... We must dispute the assumption of Roscher and Mansbach that the Romans, with their distinction of res corporales and incorporales, meant *asset objects*, goods.... The Romans by no means drew false conclusions from this distinction of theirs, and the entire doctrine of res corporales and incorporales as asset components is, apart from the forgivable fault of identifying property with its object, by no means incorrect.[130]

From this perspective we may gain further insights using Böhm's concept of rights as forms of computation. Böhm was entirely right: assets *are* forms of computation, ways in which the value of asset objects are accounted. In fact, this is historically the way in which rights have developed: as means to account for forms of property other than the full right of property – thus, to use Böhm's conception, property in restricted bundles of the renditions of service provided by the good, not in the entirety of those renditions of service, as with full property. The varied nature of goods and services made necessary the development of a category of computation forms which enabled them all to be put on a line and valued as one complete bundle, the Roman *universitas* or *patrimonium*. Which also explains the criterion that a legal object be susceptible of economic valuation in order to be considered capable of being a legal object. Money provided the universal means of valuation, by way of pricing

---

[130] Oertmann (1891), pp. 31–34.

– *pretium*. Thus rights were the means for including objects in the inventory of assets.

Which exposes just how primitive Böhm's conception of assets actually is. Böhm could only consider the actual goods and services to be assets, and had to engage in mental gymnastics to explain the phenomenon of accounting. Rights for him were a sort of subterfuge introduced as a stopgap for our inability to include certain goods and services directly on the balance sheet. But the effort is a waste of time. Goods and services *shouldn't* be listed on the balance sheet. And computation forms are not stopgaps. They are just as important to property as to other rights, to goods the utility of which is enjoyed at present as to goods the utility of which is expected at some point in the future.

This also explains the difficulties Böhm got himself into with his peculiar concept of capital. As noted above, he refused to count anything except material goods as capital. Which left him with the need to calculate a rate of return on those goods. He argued that the value of the end product somehow determined the value of the intermediate goods. He postulated the need for a certain computation form which could accomplish this, without specifying exactly what such a form actually looked like.[131] Since he jettisoned the notion that rights had anything to do with capital, he also jettisoned the role rights play in capital accounting – the role of computation forms. He was left with the marginal utility of the end product as the only clue to the valuation of capital goods, and thus had to view those goods as a sort of lump sum drawing interest. Thus, while he was quite cognizant of the fact that valuation takes place at every

---

[131] The value that accrues to these capital goods "is nothing but the *form* (the *third* form according to my enumeration) in which an indirect future advantage enters into the computation" (Böhm-Bawerk (1962), pp. 104). The value *is* the form. But isn't the form supposed to *provide* the value?

stage of the production process, he was incapable of harnessing that knowledge to develop a subjectivist, entrepreneurial concept of capital. It would be von Mises who eventually would develop such a concept (see below).

This is why Carl Menger so violently disagreed with Böhm's conception, characterizing it as "one of the greatest errors ever committed."[132] Menger saw Böhm abandoning the subjectivist basis of economics in adopting the materialist view of capital. As Gloria-Palermo characterizes it, Böhm's approach became an exercise in "objectivation" – a steady trend away from the subjectivism characterizing Menger's original approach.[133]

Ludwig von Mises' Asset-Based Concept of Capital

This discussion provides the essential background to understand Ludwig von Mises' achievement in developing his argument about the necessity for capital accounting to the proper functioning of the economy,[134] and furthermore to understand his concept of economics as human action, with the basic category being praxeology. Von Mises' praxeology in fact is the economic mirror-image of the jurisprudential viewpoint of assets expressed above, as is his capital theory.

Consider the following:

> Economics is not about things and tangible material objects; it is about men, their meanings and actions. Goods, commodities, and wealth and all the other notions of conduct are not elements of nature; they are elements of human meaning and conduct. He who

---

[132] Schumpeter (1994), pp. 847.

[133] Gloria-Palermo (1999), pp. 39ff.

[134] In particular, with respect to the socialist calculation debate. See Mises (1935).

wants to deal with them must not look at the external world; he must search for them in the meaning of acting men.[135]

The idea of capital has no counterpart in the physical universe of tangible things. It is nowhere but in the minds of planning men. It is an element in economic calculation.[136]
Capital is a praxeological concept. It is a product of reasoning, and its place is in the human mind. It is a mode of looking at the problems of acting, a method of appraising them from the point of view of a definite plan. It determines the course of human action and is, in this sense only, a real factor. It is inescapably linked with capitalism, the market economy.
The capital concept is operative as far as men in their actions let themselves be guided by capital accounting.[137]

Economics in the Misesian version is not a physical science but an ideal one; it deals with human action and human judgement. It is the world that corresponds to Jhering's vision of economics from the viewpoint of jurisprudence.

This viewpoint finds clear expression in von Mises' definition of capital; its divergence from Böhm's should be apparent.

Today there is, among businessmen and accountants, unanimity with regard to the meaning of capital. Capital is the sum of the money equivalent of all assets minus the sum of the money equivalent of all liabilities as dedicated at a definite date to the conduct of the operations of a definite business unit. It does not matter in what these assets may consist, whether they are pieces of land, buildings, equipment, tools, goods of any kind and order, claims, receivables,

---

[135] Mises (1966), p. 92.
[136] Mises (1966), p. 514.
[137] Mises (1966), p. 515.

cash, or whatever.[138]

Two things stand out in this definition of capital. Firstly, it is not the economic goods per se that qualify as capital, but their monetary equivalent. This is the same thing as saying it is not asset objects that qualify as capital but asset components. Secondly, any asset whatever may qualify as capital as long as it contributes to the production process. Böhm's "rights and relations" may just as well qualify as capital as might material goods (or better, the asset rights of which material goods are the objects).

Nevertheless, the economists remained unsatisfied with this "businessman's" view of capital, "whose calculation refers to the whole complex of his acquisitive activities."[139] They felt they needed to construct a notion of "real capital" that they could oppose to the businessman's construct. They did so by stripping out factors such as land and cash, putting forward a definition of real capital as being produced factors of production. At bottom this is an attempt to step back from the computation forms, the monetary equivalents, in which assets are expressed in order to get at the true essence of capital. Von Mises is not impressed by their efforts:

> Now this concept of totality of the produced factors of production is an empty concept. The money equivalent of the various factors of production owned by a business unit can be determined and summed up. But if we abstract from such an evaluation in money terms, the totality of the produced factors of production is merely an enumeration of physical quantities of thousands and thousands of various goods. Such an inventory is of no use to acting. It is a description of a part of the universe in terms of technology and topography and has no reference whatever to the problems raised

---

[138] Mises (1966), p. 262.

[139] Mises (1966), p. 263.

by the endeavors to improve human well-being. We may acquiesce in the terminological usage of calling the produced factors of production capital goods. But this does not render the concept of real capital any more meaningful.[140]

Trying to get behind the asset components to the core of the matter, the actual objects, only leaves us with a physical description and strips out the value judgements: but it is precisely those value judgements as embodied in monetary valuations that enable the production process to function.

The "worst outgrowth" of this conception, in Mises' view, was to attempt from it to derive a concept of the productivity of capital. Factors of production are valued according to their market price, which reflects their role in the production process. Their value is their exchange value. Factors of production are not to be considered as some sort of interest-bearing principal. It was precisely this "productivity" view of capital that Böhm put forward. Böhm, von Mises explained,

> has once for all unmasked the fallacies of the naive productivity explanations of interest, i.e., of the idea that interest is the expression of the physical productivity of factors of production. However, Böhm-Bawerk has himself based his own theory to some extent on the productivity approach. In referring in his explanation to the technological superiority of more time-consuming, roundabout processes of production, he avoids the crudity of the naive productivity fallacies. But in fact he returns, although in a subtler form, to the productivity approach.[141]

And, as discussed above, this is the inevitable result of

---

[140] Mises (1966), p. 263.

[141] Mises (1966), pp. 527–528.

abandoning assets in favor of bare goods in constructing a theory of capital.

Conclusion

The results of this analysis should be clear enough. Economists, even Austrian economists, have not gained a clear enough insight into the juridical dimension of the phenomena with which they are dealing; this has led to confusion and dead ends. Rights are not goods; so much is clear. But they *are* assets. And *goods* are *not*. This is the lesson taught by Roman law. It has been by and large forgotten. Economists need to recover it. Böhm-Bawerk's effort at delineating the role of rights in economic life, while a worthy one, was insufficient and misleading. But its shortcomings have not been recognized. A better understanding of this work certainly bears great dividends, but only when put in the context of law and economics, Roman/German style.

APPENDIX 3: THE COMMON-LAW ORDER

Here I provide an integrated exposition of the common-law social order, showing just how different it is from the social order envisioned by the natural rights theorists. The discussion of politics, economics, and religion presupposes this order.

The common law is a complex phenomenon, having various aspects, each of which conditions and depends on the other aspects. It has a supranational dimension, as the law that stands over sovereignty and conditions it; it has a national dimension, as the law of the polity, the expression of its sovereignty in a general and non-discriminate way; and it has the dimension of spontaneous generation, as being court-evolved law.[142]

All of these dimensions are various aspects of what at bottom is a unified entity.

It first finds expression, then, in an overarching law-order, a higher law (Althusius refers to it as "natural equity" – see n. 144) providing the principles undergirding all positive law-orders. This common, universal law-order does not exist in a vacuum, or as a sort of Platonic idea transcending the legal systems of the nations, but in greater or lesser degree is interwoven into each of them. In this sense the common law is the same thing as what Stahl referred to as the doctrine of law and state.[143]

---

[142] Francis Lieber proposed the term "court-evolved law" as an improvement on the misleading term "judge-made law": *On Civil Liberty and Self-Government* (Philadelphia: J. B. Lippincott & Co., 1874³), p. 214.

[143] "The standards of law and the institutions of the state differ across

This common law stands above sovereignty and conditions sovereignty. All sovereign polities are called to implement it in the positive legal orders they shape and maintain. From this perspective, positive legal orders contain **proper law**, as opposed to common law, which is universal.[144]

---

different countries and times and being the work of man, everywhere and of necessity contain bad as well as good. There is indeed however something higher, something universal, at work in all creations of law and the state, which purposes to be consummated in all of these, the consummation or lack thereof amounting to the superiority or poverty of the same; and that is the inward unchanging essence of law and state.

"Now jurisprudence is the science of law and state as it exists in a particular time under a particular people. From this arises the demand for a higher science, having as its object this inner unchanging essence of law and state. It may be called the *doctrine of law and state*." Stahl, *Philosophical Foundations*, p. 1.

[144] "Common law (*lex communis*) has been naturally implanted by God in all men.... It is commonly called the moral law (*lex moralis*).... In this common law (*jus commune*) is set forth for all men nothing other than the general theory and practice of love, both for God and for one's neighbor..... Christ set forth two headings of this common law. The first heading pertains to the performance of our duty immediately to God, and the second to what is owed to our neighbor.... Proper law (*lex propria*) is the law that is drawn up and established by the magistrate on the basis of common law (*lex communis*) and according to the nature, utility, condition, and other special circumstances of his country. It indicates the peculiar way, means, and manner by which this natural equity among men can be upheld, observed, and cultivated in any given commonwealth. Therefore, proper law (*jus proprium*) is nothing other than the practice of this common natural law (*jus naturale*) as adapted to a particular polity. It indicates how

The opposite of the common law is the **civil law**, which is formed by absolute law-creating sovereignty, and is the creature of sovereignty. In the common-law order, sovereignty is the servant of the law and exists to implement the law. In the civil-law order, sovereignty is the creator of the law; law exists to implement the will of the sovereign, and in fact *is* the will of the sovereign.[145]

There are thus two, polar-opposite forms of sovereignty, corresponding to the two forms of law. Limited sovereignty recognizes a society of pluralistic authority structures, and mediates the relationships between them. Its goal is the formation and promotion of civil society. Absolute sovereignty recognizes no authority structures it does not itself create and control. It strives not to create a society, but an overarching organization.

The common law so conceived inspired the law-order developed over the course of centuries by Western Christendom as the corollary of limited sovereignty. It was once shared, in greater or lesser degree, by all Western polities. Especially since the French Revolution, this law-order has been superseded on the European continent by the civil law, the product of absolute sovereignty and its lawmaking effort of codification. This has led to the formation of two

---

individual citizens of a given commonwealth are able to seek and attain this natural equity. Whence it is called the servant and handmaiden of common law *(jus commune)*, and a teacher leading us to the observance of common law." Johannes Althusius, *Politica Methodice Digesta,* §§. 19, 20, 22, 30.

[145] This is not to say that civil law per se is problematic. The problem arose when the civil-law and common-law traditions diverged, in particular since the French Revolution, although the roots were already in evidence for some time beforehand. For a detailed exposition of the common law/civil law opposition and its genesis, see my *A Common Law: The Law of Nations and Western Civilization.*

Western legal traditions, the common-law and the civil-law traditions, the common-law tradition carried on by the Anglo-Saxon countries (albeit haltingly), the civil-law tradition carried on in the countries of the European continent, the vehicle being the French Revolution and its successor, the Napoleonic Empire.

This development is therefore a product of the 18th and 19th centuries. Previously, there was a fundamental unity among the legal systems of the Anglo-Saxon and continental countries of Western Europe, a unity the sight of which has been lost by reading back into history these later developments. Certainly, there were major differences, but those differences cannot be used as an excuse to ignore the fundamental unity.[146]

As the common law calls for *limited* sovereignty, it calls for *multiple* sovereigns. The basis of this order of multiple sovereigns is the **nation**.[147] Nations have the calling to establish positive legal orders, each incorporating the principles of the common law. In so doing, each nation establishes its own branch of the common law, and this national law is thus also *its* common law. From this perspective, the proper law established by the sovereign is itself common law.

As such, there is no contradiction between the universal law-order and national sovereignty. A truly universal law-order in fact

---

[146] This theme calls for a book-length exposition. In the meantime, regarding the relationship of Roman and English law one may consult Bryce's *Studies in History and Jurisprudence*, Leoni's *Freedom and the Law*, McIlwain's "English Common Law" (cf. also his *Constitutionalism: Ancient and Modern*), for starters.

[147] Stahl, *Principles of Law*, pp. 79ff; *Doctrine of State*, pp. 97ff. The understanding of nations as sovereign entities is the essence of the *jus gentium* (law of nations) tradition, the major protagonists of which were Francisco de Vitoria and Althusius. For more on this, see *A Common Law* and *The Debate that Changed the West*.

requires multiple sovereigns, because only then can it retain the criteria necessary to that universality. A universal sovereign, on the other hand, of necessity would subordinate all independent activity to its own will; it cannot abide by any independent authority; it therefore can never submit to an all-encompassing order which it itself does not control – and, since it can never subject everything to its will, there will always be unresolved conflict, never unanimity. Today this tendency is evident in the quest to establish global jurisdiction for international organizations – *universal jurisdiction*. Such is the fulfillment of the civil-law tradition.

But the common law, which stands over sovereignty, conditions it and restricts it to the maintenance of an order of freedom and equality for non-sovereign, private entities. It is thus *universally integrating*. In this law-order, sovereignty serves to implement the principles of universal law in the particular legal order of the nation.

The expression of the common law in the life of the nation is the regime of **private law**. Private law is the law of liberty and equality. In it, legal persons are equals; with it, there is no respect of persons. It does not subordinate legal persons to a higher order or purpose but instead allows them to pursue their own purposes; it integrates these persons as equals, coordinating them over against each other rather than subordinating the one to the other or treating them as subordinates of a greater whole. It thus strives not for an order of monolithic organization but one of a plurality of associations.[148]

In a common-law society, there are therefore a plethora of legal persons – associations, and individuals through associations – pursuing independent goals, coordinated in terms of the integrating

---

[148] Private law as integrating common law was a major theme of Herman Dooyeweerd's sociology of law. See my article "Dooyeweerd and the Common Law" at http://84.80.12.175/commonlawreview/the-paradigm/dooyeweerd-and-the-common-law/

private law. Each of these associations, in turn, has an *internal* order governed by the principle of **distributive justice**, in which distributions are made rather than transactions, in which the members are apportioned shares and responsibilities, rights and duties, in accordance with the administrative will.

These associations are both private and public, ranging from the family to corporations, clubs, foundations, and then also to public communities such as towns, cities, and states. They all are governed by internal laws. Outwardly, they are coordinated and integrated with other associations in terms of private law. The common law *qua* private law *integrates* these activities in terms of the principle of **commutative justice**.

It is of the utmost importance to realize both the difference between distributive and commutative justice, and the mutuality thereof. The besetting sin of left and right in the modern age has been to subordinate and even subsume the one principle to the other, leading to collectivism on the one hand and individualism on the other.

The concept of justice is fundamental here and requires closer attention. The classic definition is "rendering to each his due," ensuring that what one has coming to him, one actually receives. The Roman jurist Ulpian's celebrated definition is: "Iustitia est constans et perpetua voluntas ius suum cuique tribuens" (Justice is the constant and perpetual will to render to each his due). Yet this would seem to define the just will rather than justice in itself.

Aristotle went further,[149] first making the important point that justice always concerns outward dealings with others rather than internal states of mind or mood – justice therefore always involves relations. He then took the decisive step of dividing justice into the two forms of distributive and commutative. Distributive justice is

---

[149] *Nicomachean Ethics,* ch. 5.

"exercised in the distribution of honor, wealth, and the other divisible assets of the community, which may be allotted among its members in equal or unequal shares." Commutative justice, on the other hand, "supplies a corrective principle in private transactions."

The important thing to notice here is that commutative justice is *transactional* justice. It is "no respecter of persons;" it strives to abstract the thing from the person and focus simply on the justice involved in the transaction at hand. Distributive justice, on the other hand, does not concern transactions but commands: it is realized when the person is taken into account in an appropriate manner, looking to the need or merit of the various actors. Commutative justice concerns the thing; distributive justice concerns the person.

Yet Aristotle's distinction does not quite get to the bottom of the issue. Which is, that what really is being distinguished here is *two dimensions of association*, one *internal*, the other *external*. As H. B. Acton pointed out,[150] distributive justice requires a distributing agency to be set over the persons involved in the distribution. So, the parties are subordinate to a higher decision-making authority. In commutative justice, the parties are coordinated over against each other in independence, and stand on equal terms rather than being subordinated into a higher relation. Thus, distributive justice pertains to internal order, order *within* a particular organization, while commutative justice pertains to external order, order *between* organizations.

This understanding corrects the impression given by an exclusive emphasis on the principle of methodological individualism. For there is no isolated individual standing over against society, in all his autonomous glory. There is rather the *citizen ideal*.[151] The citizen

---

[150] *The Morals of Markets and Related Essays*, p. 103.

[151] See *A Common Law,* ch. 3, "The Subject of Liberty: The Citizen."

functions not in isolation but within the associationalism of the common-law order. The individual's relationships are *mediated*, precisely through the associations of which society is composed. The citizen is the natural individual taking on the guises provided by the various associations of which he forms part. The key to properly-functioning citizenship is responsible membership in the various associations, some of which are natural and/or obligatory. One such example is the family, into which all are born. Another is the state, of which all are members (citizenship strictly speaking), with rights and responsibilities corresponding to that membership.[152] For an association to remain healthy, its members must recognize its authority over them, recognize their place in it, and pursue the shared interest of that association. In the state association, that shared interest is the *common good*.[153]

Since the sovereign does not impose the law but receives it, the common law in its guise of (external) private law is not imposed but rather issues forth, precisely as a function of the relations of the differentiated society. It results from the interactions of the independent loci of authority which are allowed to arise when sovereignty is exercised as oversight rather than command. This common law therefore grows with society; it expands as society differentiates. A primitive society lacks much in the way of a common law because most relations are internal to the associations of which it is composed; these associations are monolithic. It is therefore no accident

---

[152] For her part, the church is done an injustice when she is viewed as a voluntary organization. She is the body of Christ, membership of which is gained through baptism, bestowed upon believers and their children. Members may disavow the church's claim over them but cannot efface it. Covenants are indissoluble.

[153] See Dooyeweerd, *New Critique of Theoretical Thought,* vol. III, pp. 442ff.

that primitive societies stand in isolation and have difficulty in maintaining open communications with the outside world. They have little concept of a universal law governing such relations.

Directly, the common law governs the relations between associations, and between individuals to the degree that they act as legal persons outside of the boundaries of any particular association. *Within* associations it governs relations only indirectly, that is, to the degree that internal affairs impinge on the functioning of the common-law order. For example, contracts establishing arrangements contrary to the institutions of the universal common law (e.g., polygamy, same-sex marriage) are impermissible.

Being a function of commutative justice, these relations are of the order of transactions. Since associations pursue independent goals, they do not attempt to subordinate other associations, but only to obtain from those other associations resources which they might need the better to attain their own goals. These transactions can take on numerous forms, and can have numerous objects; they can however be summarized in the term obligation – commitments to performance.

Although there are two basic forms of obligation, contract and tort (Aristotle characterized these as voluntary and involuntary, respectively), contract is its example par excellence.[154] Contract establishes a commitment to some duty or performance. Contracts mainly involve the transfer either of goods or of services. In the case of goods, either a sale or some form of lease is contemplated; in the case of services, a commitment to do something or abstain from doing something.

Such obligation calls the concept of private property into existence. Private property only comes about in connection with these relations between legal persons. The contracts which arrange for a

---

[154] Stahl, *Private Law,* p. 100.

transfer of goods require the concept of property as a presupposition. Property, in turn, presupposes the existence of entities outside the owning group. The concept of property has no significance within the holding community, only outside of it – for everything within is held in common or in trust and is subject to the regime of distribution rather than exchange. Furthermore, property is all the goods and services at the disposal of the group, thus not only material things but also the "human capital," the capacities of members capable of being put to profitable use and in demand on the part of those outside. All of these can be leveraged. See the chapter on economics for a more thorough explanation of this.

The common law as external private law develops in terms of these inter-group arrangements, reciprocally influencing their development and being influenced by it. The point of contact of this development is the judiciary, the adjudicative branch of government. This is one of the main instruments through which sovereignty affects the social order. By rendering decisions in cases of dispute, the judiciary confirms valid forms of relation, and of the components of relation. These "jural relations" as they are sometimes known are *rights*, involving both legal persons (individuals and associations) and legal objects (goods and services).

Rights, as shown in the chapter on politics, are derived through the process of cultural amelioration. As civilization advances, individuals, in line with the doctrine of subjective right, become more empowered; at the same time groups, in particular the family, evolve from monolithic units of control into facultative auxiliaries. But this is only possible as the individual assumes greater levels of personal responsibility. Freedom requires responsibility; without it, subjection is required, for where personal responsibility is not exercised, the alternative to subjection is anarchy.

The common law as a universe of burgeoning rights thus develops in the service of a spontaneous order. It facilitates relations between groups by bringing to bear the legal institutions which can mediate those relations. These institutions include property, contract, tort or delict, due process of law, legal personality. They are not imposed, but rather grow out of custom and prescription as recognized by the courts.[155] However, they are implicit in the logic of the common law. [156] Such relations will always be conducted through such legal institutions, wherever such relations arise.

In this process, the courts are determined by precedent and thus follow a given trajectory, although such determination is not rigid; they are guided forward by the inner logic of the common law as entailed in its capacity as a universal, integrating legal order showing itself no respecter of persons – in other words, treating all persons

---

[155] Maine summarized the process of the growth of common law in this manner: "Ancient jurisprudence, if a perhaps deceptive comparison may be employed, may be likened to International Law, filling nothing, as it were, excepting the interstices between the great groups which are the atoms of society. In a community so situated, the legislation of assemblies and the jurisdiction of Courts reaches only to the heads of families, and to every other individual the rule of conduct is the law of his home, of which his Parent is the legislator. But the sphere of civil law, small at first, tends steadily to enlarge itself. The agents of legal change, Fictions, in turn to bear on the Equity, and Legislation, are brought primeval institutions, and at every point of the progress, a greater number of personal rights and a larger amount of property are removed from the domestic forum to the cognisance of the public tribunals. The ordinances of the government obtain gradually the same efficacy in private concerns as in matters of state, and are no longer liable to be overridden by the behests of a despot enthroned by each hearthstone." *Ancient Law,* pp. 147–148.

[156] The inner logic of common law (external private law) is explored in Ernest J. Weinrib, *The Idea of Private Law* (Cambridge: Harvard University Press, 1995).

equally. Here the common law reveals itself as general equity. Therefore, courts operating in terms of custom and equity as so defined
act, in the issuing of decisions, as determinators of value, of the
norms by which society is ruled. They do so not by prescribing a law
but by providing an interpretation on the basis of received law
which then gives to law and custom its boundaries and indicates its
path forward into the future (so-called path dependency). Decisions and precedents are the framework through which the common law takes shape in a particular society.

The values of society are therefore fundamentally influenced by
the decisions issued by the courts. The legal system takes shape upon
this basis, and legislation, if it is to maintain the legal order of the
common law, must respect this legal system and build upon it.[157] In
the civil-law approach, legislation becomes omnipotent and takes it
upon itself to replace this customary order. In so doing it interrupts
the continuity of a society with its past and introduces an artificial-
ity and an uprootedness which has a thoroughly pernicious effect
on societal mores.[158]

This is the process by which, in a common-law order, valuation
takes place which is valid across the society. Valuation occurs
through a process in which an appeal is made to sovereign (or the
sovereign's representative) to adjudicate on a point of uncertainty.
It is this decision which is decisive because it then becomes binding

---

[157] This is the meaning behind the Historical School of Jurisprudence's in-
sistence on custom as the basis of law, and the need for jurisprudence and
legislation to recognize and take into account that basis in further legal
development. See Stahl, *Principles of Law,* pp. 49ff.; Savigny, *System of the
Modern Roman Law,* vol. I, §§. 7ff. (An updated, corrected version is available at http://84.80.12.175/commonlawreview/juridical/savigny-on-
principles-of-law.)

[158] This is detailed in *Common Law & Natural Rights.*

on society at large; it becomes law. And the law, as Stahl has noted, "is the primary, most immediate ethical measure for the actions of men;"[159] as such, it has a ripple effect throughout society, influencing its very moral fiber, for better or for worse.

We can therefore establish as the fundamental theorem of the common-law order the following formula: the *sovereign confirmation,* under the *leading of justice* and *in line with precedent,* of *(external) social value, in response to request, at the margin.*

- Sovereign confirmation: a binding decision made by the public authority, enforced by the power of that authority, that cannot be gainsaid.
- The leading of justice: this decision is arrived at in strict consultation with the principle of justice.
- In line with precedent: this decision is correlated with previous decisions pertaining to the matter at hand; it must be shown to follow those decisions, or, if necessary, to derogate from them, and how; such derogation carries the burden of proof.
- Social value: valuation which is "current," i.e., which is valid for society at large, and not just within a particular family or other group; as such, it is imparted to all, and all are held accountable to it.
- In response to request: decisions are arrived at by appeal to authority, they are not handed down by decree. As such, they spring from the grass roots, from living reality, and capture the spontaneous development of society.
- At the margin: decisions are made only regarding a fraction of conflicts and other situations of doubt, and provide guidance to actors as to how to conform future behavior.

---

[159] Stahl, *Principles of Law,* p. 39.

This process implements and generates the integrating universal value structure upon which civilization rests, which is the common law.

It integrates the universal with the particular, top-down with bottom-up.

The common law therefore brings down the higher law, which is God's will for human society, into the life of the nation by means of the instrumentality of sovereignty, which through a process of spontaneous ordering overseen by the state generates the pluralist, differentiated, associationalist order characterized by liberty under law, and upheld by individuals dedicated to the citizen ideal.

BIBLIOGRAPHY

Acton, H. B. *The Morals of Markets and Related Essays.* Indianapolis: Liberty Fund, 1993.

Alvarado, Ruben. *A Common Law: The Law of Nations and Western Civilization.* Second edition. Aalten: WordBridge Publishing, 2019 [1999].

—. *Calvin and the Whigs: A Study in Historical Political Theology.* Aalten: Pantocrator Press, 2017.

—. *Common Law & Natural Rights: The Question of Conservative Foundations.* Aalten: WordBridge Publishing, 2009.

—. *Follow the Money: The Money Trail through History.* Aalten: WordBridge Publishing, 2013.

—. *Investing in the New Normal: Beyond the Keynesian Endpoint.* Aalten: WordBridge Publishing, 2010.

—. *The Debate that Changed the West: Grotius versus Althusius.* Aalten: Pantocrator Press, 2018.

Bellomo, Manlio. *The Common Legal Past of Europe 1000–1800,* trans. Lydia G. Cochrane. Washington, DC: The Catholic University Press of America, 1995.

Berman, Harold. *Law and Revolution: The Formation of the Western Legal Tradition.* Cambridge, MA: Harvard University Press, 1983.

Böhm-Bawerk, Eugen von. *Rechte und Verhältnisse vom Standpunkte der volkswirthschaftlichen Güterlehre: Kritische Studie* [Rights and Relations from the Standpoint of the Goods Doctrine of Economics]. Innsbruck: Verlag der Wagner'schen Universitäts-Buchhandlung, 1881.

—. "Whether Legal Rights and Relationships are Economic Goods," trans. George D. Huncke, in *Shorter Classics of Eugen von Böhm-Bawerk, Vol. 1.* South Holland, IL: Libertarian Press, 1962.

Bryce, James. *Studies in History and Jurisprudence.* New York: Oxford University Press, 1901.

Chalmers, Thomas. *On Political Economy, In Connexion With the Moral State and Moral Prospects of Society.* Glasgow: William Collins, 1832.

—. *Problems of Poverty: Selections from the Economic and Social Writings of Thomas Chalmers D.D.,* arr. Henry Hunter. London et al.: Thomas Nelson & Sons, n.d.

Dankwardt, H. *Nationalökonomisch-civilistische Studiën* [Studies in Economics and Roman Law]. Leipzig and Heidelberg: C. F. Winter'sche Verlagshandlung, 1862.

Eliot, T. S. *The Idea of a Christian Society.* London: Faber and Faber Limited, 1939.

Endres, A.M. *Neoclassical Economic Theory: the Founding Austrian Version.* London and New York: Routledge, 1997.

Gierke, Otto von. *Natural Law and the Theory of Society 1500–1800,* trans. with an introduction by Ernest Barker. Cambridge: University Press, 1934.

Gloria-Palermo, Sandye. *Evolution of Austrian Economics: From Menger to Lachmann.* London and New York: Routledge, 1999.

Grotius, Hugo. *De Jure Belli ac Pacis Libri Tres,* trans. Francis W. Kelsey. Oxford: At the Clarendon Press, 1925.

Haines, Charles Grove. *The Revival of Natural Law Concepts: A Study of the Establishment and of the Interpretation of Limits on Legislatures with special reference to the Development of certain phases of American Constitutional Law.* Cambridge, MA: Harvard University Press, 1930.

Heinsohn, Gunnar, and Otto Steiger. *Eigentum, Zins und Geld: Ungelöste Rätsel der Wirtschaftswissenschaft* [Property, Interest, and Money: Unsolved Mysteries of Economic Science], fourth, revised edition. Marburg: Metropolis Verlag, 2006.

—. "Property Titles as the Clue to a Successful Transformation," in *Verpflichtungsökonomik: Eigentum, Freiheit und Haftung in der*

Geldwirtschaft [Obligation Economics: Property, Freedom, and Liability in the Money Economy], ed. Gunnar Heinsohn and Otto Steiger. Marburg: Metropolis Verlag, 2001.

—. "The Property Theory of Interest and Money," in *What Is Money?* ed. John Smithin. London: Routledge, 2000.

Hoedemaker, P. J. *Article 36 of the Belgic Confession Vindicated against Dr. Abraham Kuyper.* Aalten: Pantocrator Press, 2019.

Huizinga, Johan. *Dutch Civilisation in the 17th Century and other essays.* London: The Fontana Library, 1968.

Kuyper, Abraham. *De Gemeene Gratie.* Kampen: J. H. Kok, 1902–1904.

—. *Lectures on Calvinism.* Grand Rapids, MI: Wm. B. Eerdmans Publishing Co., 1931 [1898].

—. *Vrijheid.* Amsterdam: H. de Hoogh & Co., 1873.

Jhering, Rudolph von. *Geist des römischen Rechts auf den verschiedenen Stufen seiner Entwicklung.* Leipzig: Breitkopf und Härtel, 1874.

Justinian, Emperor. *Institutes.* Vol. II of *The Civil Law,* translated, edited, etc. by S.P. Scott A.M. Cincinnati: The Central Trust Company, 1932.

Lachmann, Ludwig. *Capital and its Structure.* London: G. Bell and Sons, Ltd, 1956.

Leoni, Bruno. *Freedom and the Law.* Los Angeles: Nash Publishing, 1972 [1961].

Locke, John. *Two Treatises of Government,* in *The Works, vol. 4: Economic Writings and Two Treatises of Government.* 12th edition. London: Rivington, 1824.

Macleod, Henry Dunning. *The Elements of Economics.* London: Longmans, Green, and Co., 1881.

—. *The Elements of Political Economy.* London: Longman, Brown, Green, Longmans, and Roberts, 1858.

Maine, Henry Sumner. *Ancient Law.* London: John Murray, 1908 [1861].

Malthus, Thomas Robert. *An Essay on the Principle of Population.* London: J. Johnson, 1798.

McIlwain, Charles Howard. *Constitutionalism: Ancient and Modern.* Ithaca NY, et al.: Cornell University Press, 1940.

—. "The English Common Law, Barrier Against Absolutism." *The American Historical Review,* Vol. 49, No. 1. (Oct., 1943), pp. 23–31.

Menger, Carl. *Principles of Economics* [Grundsätze der Volkswirtschaftslehre]. Vienna: Wilhelm Braumüller, 1871.

Mises, Ludwig von. "Economic Calculation in the Socialist Commonwealth." In *Collectivist Economic Planning,* pp. 87–130. London: George Routledge & Sons, 1935.

—. *Human Action: A Treatise on Economics.* Third revised edition. Chicago: Henry Regnery Company, 1966.

North, Gary. *Political Polytheism: The Myth of Pluralism.* Tyler, TX: Institute for Christian Economics, 1989.

Novak, Michael. *The Spirit of Democratic Capitalism.* New York: Touchstone, 1982.

Oertmann, Paul. *Die Volkswirtschaftslehre des Corpus Juris Civilis.* Berlin: Prager, 1891.

Penn, William, "England's Present Interest Considered," in *The Political Writings of William Penn,* ed. Andrew R. Murphy. Indianapolis: Liberty Fund, 2002.

Perry, Richard L. (ed.). *Sources of Our Liberties: Documentary Origins of Individual Liberties in the United States Constitution and Bill of Rights.* Chicago: American Bar Foundation, 1978.

Polanyi, Karl, *The Great Transformation.* New York: Farrar & Rinehart, Inc., 1944.

Polyander, Johan, et al. *Synopsis purioris theologiae, disputationibus quinquaginta duabus comprehensa.* Ed. Dr. H. Bavinck. Leyden: Donner, 1881 [1625].

Rousseau, Jean-Jacques. *Discourse on Inequality,* in *The Basic Political Writings,* trans. Donald A. Cress. Indianapolis, Indiana: Hackett Publishing Company, 1987.

Ruler, A. A. van. *Religie en Politiek.* Nijkerk: G. F. Callenbach, 1945.

Rushdoony, Rousas John. *Politics of Guilt and Pity.* Fairfax VA: Thoburn Press, 1978 [1970].

—. *This Independent Republic: Studies in the Nature and Meaning of American History.* Fairfax VA: Thoburn Press, 1978 [1965].

Savigny, Friedrich Carl von. *System of the Modern Roman Law,* trans, William Holloway. Madras: J. Higginbotham, 1867.

Schumpeter, Joseph. *History of Economic Analysis.* Ed. Elizabeth Boody Schumpeter. London: Routledge, 1994 [1954].

—. "Schumpeter on Böhm-Bawerk." In *The Development of Economic Thought: Great Economists in Perspective,* ed. Henry William Spiegel, pp. 568–589. New York: J. Wiley, 1952.

Smith, Adam. *An Inquiry into the Nature and Causes of the Wealth of Nations.* London: Methuen and Co., Ltd., ed. Edwin Cannan, 1904.

Soto, Hernando de. *The Other Path: The Invisible Revolution in the Third World.* New York: Harper & Row, 1989.

—. *The Mystery of Capital: Why Capitalism Triumphs in the West and Fails Everywhere Else.* New York: Basic Books, 2000.

Stadermann, Hans-Joachim, and Otto Steiger. *Schulökonomik: Allgemeine Theorie der Wirtschaft, Band 1* [The Economics of the Schools: General Theory of Economics, Volume 1]. Tübingen: Mohr Siebeck, 2001.

Stahl, Friedrich Julius. *Philosophical Foundations.* Aalten: WordBridge Publishing, 2022.

—. *Principles of Law,* translated, edited, and introduced by Ruben Alvarado. Aalten: WordBridge Publishing, 2007.

—. *Private Law,* translated, edited, and introduced by Ruben Alvarado. Aalten: WordBridge Publishing, 2007.

—. *The Doctrine of State & the Principles of State Law,* translated, edited, and introduced by Ruben Alvarado. Aalten: WordBridge Publishing, 2009.

—. *The Rise and Fall of Natural Law,* translated, edited, and prefaced by Ruben Alvarado. Aalten: WordBridge Publishing, 2020.

Steuart, James. *An Inquiry into the Principles of Political Economy*, in *The Works, Political, Metaphysical, and Chronological, of the Late Sir James Steuart of Coltness, Bart.* London: Cadell & Davies, 1805.

Tellenbach, Gert. *Church, State, and Christian Society at the Time of the Investiture Contest,* transl. R. F. Bennett. Oxford: Blackwell, 1940.

Weston, Corinne C. "England: Ancient Constitution and Common Law," in *The Cambridge History of Political Thought: 1450–1700,* edited by J. H. Burns with the assistance of Mark Goldie. Cambridge: Cambridge University Press, 1991.

INDEX

Lightning Source UK Ltd.
Milton Keynes UK
UKHW020837130123
415295UK00018B/1722